Beneath the Southern Cross

Daniel Snider

ISBN 978-1-68570-431-5 (paperback)
ISBN 978-1-68570-432-2 (digital)

Christian Faith Publishing
832 Park Avenue
Meadville, PA 16335
www.christianfaithpublishing.com

Printed in the United States of America

Introduction

This is a story about primitive people, their customs, and their need for peace and happiness. This story is about a young couple who wanted to share the gospel of Christ with primitive people. This is a fiction novel, not about the people who are already serving in the jungles of Papua New Guinea. I have to apologize to the veteran missionaries who have served in this area. I have never been to Australia or to Papua New Guinea. I have done some mission work in Mexico and in the Philippines, but these people and these circumstances are situations I have personally never been part of. However, I have read about these encounters with those Stone Age people and have even met some of the missionaries who worked with them.

This fictional couple we will be telling you about had already heard about these people through literature they had read. They had met some missionaries who worked in Papua New Guinea, and they were willing to do the work God was calling them to do. They knew God wants everyone on earth to hear His gospel of salvation; it was their plan to try to reach out to people who had never heard that good news. But their hearts were touched when they had missionaries come to their church, sharing the difficulties of reaching out to primitive people and translating that primitive language so these people could actually hear and learn to read God's amazing message.

And now the story begins…

1
Chapter

Departure

"You have finished your course of study here. It is my hope that you will be able to take what you have learned into some worthy project. Some of you will be going to distant lands to live in the midst of strange surroundings to accomplish your goals. And, speaking of goals, let me urge you to set them high, for you will certainly not attain any level higher than the pinnacle of your dreams.

"Go now to your endeavors with enthusiasm, and I pray, with God's blessing. Goodbye and may God be with you."

Professor Murlet's final admonition rang in Hal's thoughts as Brother Harris's car carried the Fosters to the airport. Hal and Winnie Foster were actually on their way! They were going to the mission field. Their books and most of their clothes and personal belongings, that is, those things that survived the culling process, were already on the way to New Guinea. Those items had been sent weeks ago in a crate, which had been shipped from the dock at Toronto.

"Hal, look at the marker Mrs. Frederick gave to me before we left the church."

Winnie's voice broke through Hal's musings. "That's nice, honey," Hal replied as he looked at the crocheted cross tucked between the pages of Winnie's Bible. It was white, with a light-blue border all the way around and the words *Drew Chapel* down the vertical beam.

"I'll sure miss those people at Drew Chapel," Winnie said as a tear found its way to her cheek.

"Yes," thought Hal, "we'll both miss them. Miss them a lot."

They were just passing the avenue they had traveled so many times these past several months on their way to their linguistics classes at the University of Toronto. *I wonder when we'll get back here,* Hal thought. It seemed like only last week since they had left the little church in Montana to go to a linguistics school. Now they were on their way to New Guinea.

The car slowed as it made the turn toward the airport terminal. "Well, we're just about there," Doug Harris said, turning his head slightly to cast a glance at Hal in the front seat and Winnie in the rear seat. "I don't know what I'm going to do without the two of you at the church. You were a godsend to us. Your enthusiasm for serving the Lord has breathed new life into the entire congregation. If you have half the effect on New Guinea that you've had in our church, the whole island will be Christian in just a few years."

Doug was the minister at Drew Chapel. He and his wife, Karen, had been there for six years and had been near the point of giving up on their efforts with the church when the Fosters had arrived in Toronto to go to the linguistics school. Hal and Winnie had become active in the church from the very week of their arrival, and their support of Doug's ministry had been just the encouragement that was needed. Now the Drew Chapel church was acting as forwarding agent for the Fosters and had provided their travel funds to New Guinea, as well as a large portion of their needed living-link financial support on the mission field.

Yes, the Fosters' presence at Drew Chapel had been quite a blessing. Now the church had a higher goal than ever before, and they felt a very strong sense of participation in the effort to win the world for Christ while there was still time.

Doug looked at Hal as they stood in the terminal waiting for the Fosters' flight to arrive. Hal was not tall by American standards.

He stood a good two inches shorter than Doug's six feet, but he was sturdily built. Hal was handsome in a rugged sort of way. He looked like he would be at home in a mining camp or a lumber mill, although when dressed in a three-piece suit, he would not have been out of place in a bank office. *A man among men. At least he will be when he's had more time to mature*, Doug thought as he observed Hal's calmness in preparing to board the plane.

Boarding and departure took about forty-five minutes, but it didn't seem that long because everyone was trying to squeeze in as much talk as possible in their final moments together. Tears had flowed profusely as lumps in throats were being valiantly swallowed. It's not easy to leave the ones you love behind, and it is neither easy for those left behind to see you leave. Winnie hated the weakness that blurred her vision so that she could not clearly make out her friends standing in the terminal window as the plane taxied past on its way for takeoff. Soon they were aloft, leaving Toronto behind.

"Hal, there's snow on the mountains down there. Can we be flying over Montana?"

"No, we must be over Colorado. On a nonstop flight to Los Angeles, we wouldn't be far enough north to fly over Montana."

Montana, Hal thought wistfully. He had always thought there could be no more beautiful place on all the earth than the Montana Rockies. Hal and his dad had trekked over much of that mountain terrain as they backpacked into the high country for the wilderness hunting and the fishing they both loved. Hal had learned to carry a sixty-pound pack for a full day at a time, and then another day after that on their hiking and camping trips.

Thoughts of Montana triggered emotions in Winnie too. No, not the backpacking trips although she had learned to enjoy the wilderness with her rugged, outdoor-loving husband. Winnie now remembered the missions rally at their little church in Billings. Ed and Mary Hart had come for that rally, and before they left, both Hal and Winnie felt a burning within their souls to help take the gospel to the people of New Guinea. The Harts were involved in Bible translation and evangelism among the primitive tribes of that distant land. There were so many tribes that had never heard the Lord's gospel in any language, much less in their own.

Within a year of the missions rally, after much prayer and seeking after the Lord's will, Hal had resigned as minister of the little church in Billings to prepare for the mission field.

Winnie was so lost in thought she did not notice as Hal turned his head to study her. *What a beauty I married*, he thought. Indeed, she was pretty; light-brown hair fell loosely to her shoulders. Her complexion was smooth with a scattering of a few small freckles. She had a medium build for her medium height, and her quick movements spoke of someone with plenty of energy.

The stewardess's voice brought both Hal and Winnie's thoughts abruptly to the present. "Ladies and gentlemen, we will be landing in Los Angeles in about fifteen minutes. We hope you have enjoyed your flight on Braniff Airlines today. Please put all carry-on luggage beneath the seat in front of you and fasten your seat belts for landing."

The flight had taken over four hours, but it had seemed like less time had passed since leaving Toronto. If their flight out of Los Angeles was on time, they would be out over the Pacific and on their long journey away from everything that was familiar to them. A few hours in the terminal in Los Angeles would enable them to walk out some of the weariness before that long flight ahead.

2
Chapter

Papua

Hal bounced in his seat, and jolted, woke with a start. The captain's voice came over the plane's intercom system saying they were experiencing some turbulence from a thunderstorm over the Pacific. Looking out the window, he saw the massive cloud tower beside the plane that was the cause of the rough flying conditions.

"Look, Winnie!" Hal exclaimed as he shook his dozing wife awake. Winnie blinked her eyes open and rolled her head against the back of the seat to see what Hal was indicating with his outstretched hand.

He's just like a little boy in his excitement over this grand adventure, thought Winnie.

"Look at the light show God has arranged for us, Winnie," Hal said. And a light show it was. The powerful surges of the electrical storm in the clouds enabled the passengers of the airplane to clearly see the formation of the clouds in the night sky, lighted columns flashing on with such rapidity that the sky was not dark for even a moment.

Again, the captain's voice came over the speakers, "If you have never witnessed a tropical thunderstorm before, you're probably amazed at all the colors you see in these lighted clouds. This phenomenon can be seen throughout the tropics but will never be seen just quite like this in the temperate zones of the world."

Hal and Winnie were amazed at the brilliant colors and watched the atmospheric display with wonder. It far surpassed any theatrical light show at any rock concert. The explosions of light in the cloud mass brought gasps of delight from the other passengers. Never had the Fosters seen anything comparable to this brilliant array of beauty, although they would see many more such displays in the years to come in their new tropical home.

As the plane continued on, leaving the flashing clouds behind, Winnie leaned against the backrest of her seat with a sigh. The sleep she had been enjoying before it was interrupted by the thunderstorm had not completely satisfied the weariness that now engulfed her. "Hal," she said, "I didn't think I would get this tired so soon."

"It must be jet lag," Hal replied.

They had been in the air for several hours since leaving the Honolulu airport. The short layover in Honolulu had not afforded much time to rest before boarding the flight for Sidney, Australia. Hal's legs were beginning to feel numb, so he stretched them as much as possible and shifted his weight in the seat to ease the discomfort of sitting in one position for so long.

Looking out the window into the darkness, he thought he noticed the beginnings of dawn over the ocean. Yes, there definitely was the line of the horizon being slightly lighted by the first faint rays of the morning. Suddenly, brilliant light fairly burst above the waves far below. The sunrise seemed to come much more suddenly when flying at forty thousand feet over the Pacific than it did two thousand miles inland while surrounded by mountain peaks.

"Prepare for landing soon," said the Australian stewardess with that Australian-accented English. "We are descending for our landing at Sidney, Australia. Please place any handbags or loose objects under your feet and fasten your seat belts. We want to thank you for flying Qantas and hope you have had a pleasant journey."

The change of planes at Sidney was so fast the Fosters had to hurry through the terminal to board the smaller airliner that would take them the last distance to their destination. The small size of the craft in comparison to the huge 707 that had carried them on their transcontinental journey did not detract from its comfort. It was actually a nicer cabin than that of the larger plane. Of course, Hal and Winnie were not in the first-class seating in the 707 from Honolulu to Sidney.

Hal began to tap the armrest of his seat nervously. So near, yet so far to go. These last few hours were the worst of the entire trip because of that nervousness, not because of the accommodations but because of his anticipation of what was in store for them. Looking out across the wing, Hal could see land looming up before them and mountains in the distance.

"That can't be snow!" exclaimed Winnie as she saw some white on the peaks in the distance.

"Well, it might be," said Hal. "They have some very high mountains in New Guinea. Although it certainly won't be like Montana."

"The land is so big. I pictured New Guinea as an island, but the coast just goes on and on and on. I guess it really must be the second largest island in the world!"

Hal chuckled at Winnie's outburst. He, too, was not quite prepared for the mass before them that looked very much like a continent from their viewpoint. The horizon stretched as far as the eye could see, even from their vantage point of several thousand feet of elevation as the plane neared their destination.

As the landing gear touched down on the runway at Port Moresby, Hal thought, *New Guinea! We're finally here!* Excitement welled up inside him in spite of his resolve to remain calm. They could see from their window that Port Moresby, Papua, New Guinea, was a modern city. It seemed to bely the fact that not too many land miles distant was a primitive jungle inhabited by Stone Age tribes. An involuntary chill ran up Hal's back as he anticipated the beginning of their work on this dreamed-of mission field.

"There's Ed and Mary!" squealed Winnie, and she hurried down the steps of the loading ramp, nearly losing her balance as she tripped over the last step. With Hal close behind, she rushed into Mary's waiting embrace. Hugs, hearty handshakes, and customs inspections later, they strode toward the waiting Toyota minibus, with all available hands gripping the handles of suitcases and travel bags. Excited chatter filled the early morning air as they loaded the Fosters' belongings into the van before setting off to join the other missionaries.

"The others are anxious to meet you," said Ed as he started the van's engine. "We knew there just wouldn't be enough room for everyone who wanted to come to meet you, and all of your luggage too. There are nine of us, you know. Bob and Sally Merchant have a little eight-year-old boy, Barry, and Sid and Molly Craft have two children. Sandie is twelve, and Jamie is seven. Jamie is our true native New Guinean. He was born here."

Arriving at a large, rambling white stucco house, the group laughed as they saw a blond-haired youngster come bursting out of the door, falling over a toy wagon, and leaping to his feet as if nothing had happened to slow his progress to meet them. "That's Barry," Mary said with a laugh. "He's so lively. The natives back in the bush think he's really special because of his blonde hair. I'm afraid he might be just a little spoiled with all the attention the natives give him, but he's really easy to love."

Winnie could see right off that Barry was easy to love. His bright smile spread over the entirety of his face and erupted into a toothy grin as he realized they were laughing over his exuberant tumble over the toy wagon.

Almost immediately, more faces appeared in the doorway of the house. Two young women and an almost teenage girl came down the three steps from the porch. One of the women was short and somewhat round, with her long dark hair pulled back to a single braid that queued down her back. The other woman was tall, taller than even the average man. Her complexion was light, going well with her blue eyes and blonde Dutch boy cut hair.

"Sally, Molly, this is our new family, Hal and Winnie Foster," Mary called as she opened the door of the van to step to the ground. Winnie already had their names matched to their faces. Sally was the tall blonde. She was obviously the mother of the mischievous Barry. Molly had all the warmth of a molly. Winnie couldn't help but compare her to a cuddly Raggedy Ann doll. The ladies were quickly involved in busy chatter, and Winnie knew she was going to enjoy her association with these dedicated missionary families.

"Sid had to go to town already this morning to arrange for delivery of some of our supplies later today, but Bob's out back, working on the Land Rover," Sally said to Ed. "You will probably want to take Hal back there to meet him."

"Are you a good mechanic?" asked Ed as he led Hal around the side of the house to where all they could see of Bob was a very long pair of legs, the upper body being bent over the engine of the truck. "Bob, we have a visitor," said Ed as he and Hal drew nearer. Then out from under the hood of the vehicle uncoiled one of the tallest men Hal had ever met. Bob's face was half covered by a thick thatch of brown beard, and the exposed patches of skin were smudged with dirt and grease. The face lifted into a smile, and Bob wiped greasy hands on a rag. "You must be Hal," he grinned.

Even through the beard, Hal could see where Barry came by his own big grin. "You must have been a basketball player," Hal mused as he stretched out his hand to have it engulfed in a huge hand and an enormous handshake.

"Yes, I played a little college ball at the University of Colorado. But then the Lord latched onto me, and I knew He had something more important in life for me than fun and games." With no pause he added, "I hope you're a mechanic. We have to do our own work around here, you know. It's a long way to the local garage when we're back in the bush."

"Have you found the trouble?" asked Ed, with anxious creases in his brow. "Yeah, it's the water pump. I'm sure glad we found it here instead of out there in the bush. The Lord's perfect timing has come to our rescue again." Hal silently agreed. He wondered what they did when faced with major mechanical failures when out so far from civilization.

The balance of the morning was spent with the men putting a new water pump on the Land Rover and giving the Fosters a quick tour of the house. There were supplies stacked in several rooms.

"You haven't seen anything yet. Wait until the rest of the supplies are brought out from town this afternoon. We're really going to be cluttered around here then," Bob said. "We have two weeks to get everything sorted and organized for our trip back into the bush, and we will need every day of it!"

The Fosters' crates had arrived a week before the Fosters did, and they were piled on top of one another in one of the bedrooms.

"This will be your home for the next two weeks. You will have some time to decide what you will take with you into the bush and what you'll leave behind. We'll help you." That last remark by Ed was encouraging to Winnie, but she realized that two weeks really wasn't going to be that much more than enough time to get organized for the trip into the primitive interior.

An involuntary shudder went through her as she realized how close they actually were to entering a totally different world from what they were used to. Not that she was afraid, this was what they had come for. It was just going to be so much different, and there were so many unknowns. Molly must have sensed Winnie's sudden apprehension, for she spoke softly to her, "We will use these two weeks to tell you everything we know about the culture and habits of the tribes we work with. They are really a joy, and we hardly ever feel threatened by any of them. The only thing to fear from them is their fear of us." Winnie felt herself relax a little.

Sid arrived back at the house just before lunchtime with seven-year-old Jamie in tow. "How was town, Jamie? Did you see the policeman?" Bob teased.

"Uncle Bob," Jamie excitedly cried, "we saw a big truck with a train on it scooping dirt!"

Sid laughed, "Jamie, it was a crane, not a train." To the others, he explained, "They're doing some excavating for a new high-rise building. I am still amazed at the contrast here in this land after ten years being here. Here in Port Moresby, they are just as modern as in any American city, but out there," he motioned toward the interior of the island, "it might just as well be 1880 as 1980."

The women were just getting the dishes cleared from the table following the noon meal when a delivery truck braked to a stop outside the house.

"The suppliers are here," called Sid. "Come on, fellas, it won't take long to unload it if we all help." And with four strong men and two small boys, it didn't take very long at all. Soon the entire group was busy unpacking boxes and taking the contents into the various rooms of the house as canned and dried foods were being kept in one room, hardware items in another, clothing in another, and so on.

Late on that same afternoon, an official-looking car stopped in front of the house. A uniformed man strode to the door and knocked. When Mary answered the door, the uniformed man said, "I wish to speak to Mister Edward Hart on official government business." When Ed came, the officer said, "Mister Hart, the Office of Interior would like for you to come to our Port Moresby headquarters to meet with the territorial governor. You may come with me, if you wish, and I will bring you back when we are finished."

"Why, yes, that would be very kind of you. Just let me get my hat, and I'll be right with you." Ed cast a glance at the others that said, "I don't quite know what to make of this. Pray for me while I'm gone." The official government car left while ten pairs of eyes followed its progress down the road.

"What do you make of that, Bob?" Sid asked.

"I don't know for sure," Bob replied. "I hope nothing has happened that will hinder our return to the tribes of the interior. I think we'd better have a prayer meeting on this thing."

"I agree," said Molly, and with no further discussion, the entire group went to their knees on the varnished boards of the kitchen floor.

Nearly all the veteran missionaries prayed along the same lines. Sid's prayer was representative of them all: "Lord, we know You are in control of every moment of our lives. We know You have brought us here to this strange land to do Your work, and we are willing to do it. We've come to love these bushmen with their naked bodies and hungry souls. We want nothing to hinder our ministry among them. But we also know the wiles of the devil. We know he would try anything to destroy Your work. Lord, we trust You completely to handle any problem that Ed will face in his meeting with the governor. May Your will be done. In Jesus's name, amen."

Peace settled over the group when the prayers were finished, and they resumed their sorting and packing for the following hours. They were so engrossed in their work they did not hear the car that brought Ed back into their midst. The first thing that told them that Ed was back was his greeting as he closed the screen door behind himself. "Hello! I'm back. We need to talk!"

All work stopped as all the missionaries assembled in the large kitchen. Some sat in chairs around the table. Some were too nervous to sit, and stood, but all their eyes were on Ed.

"I met with Territorial Governor Lawrence, and the interior minister. What they had to talk about had nothing to do with our work in the bush. They want to know if we can spare a family to open a new area that has been kept free from civilization's influence."

Bob interrupted, "I thought that's what we've been doing. Where's this new area? We've almost reached the border of their jurisdiction now as it is."

"This area isn't in New Guinea," Ed answered. "It's an island way out in the Pacific, but still within the boundaries of the Royal Papua New Guinea Constabulary. It has a small native population that the outside world knows nothing of. The island is a long way from any other inhabited land. It is not on modern maps because the Papuan government wanted to protect its people from the *wrong kind* of civilization. They have been able to keep its presence secret because it's so far from the shipping lanes."

"But why, if they have wanted to keep the natives from the influence of civilization, do they want someone to go in there now?" Sid asked.

"It's because they're afraid they can't always keep it a secret. They know we haven't tried to make Americans out of the natives in New Guinea. We've been careful to not try to change any of their customs that were not immoral, therefore preserving their heritage while giving them the gospel of Christ. That's the kind of influence they want for this remote island people."

"But who can we spare?" Sally's question was already in the minds of every one of the adults in the circle. The work they had begun, but not yet finished, seemed to require each of them to continue with their work. To leave a partially finished work might mean to lose all the headway they had made with those people. The Merchants had just gained a foothold with their natives, and the Crafts had been working with their present tribe a little longer, but the work was not yet ready to be left unaided. Hal and Winnie could not be expected to just pick up where either the Crafts or Merchants had left off because they had yet to learn the language. Ed and Mary needed to stay at Port Moresby for a year to work on printing the translations the teams had been working on. This discussion lasted late into the evening.

Finally, Ed, with a solemn look in his eyes and the same solemn tone in his voice, spoke: "We can't afford to give up any of the work we are now doing, but neither can we afford to pass up this open door the Lord has placed in front of us." His eyes shifted from one concerned face to another, then came to rest on Hal. "Hal, you and Winnie are the only people among us who could take on this new work without seriously endangering the other works already in progress. I know you will have to learn the language of the natives, but the language there would be new to any of us. Would you and Winnie be willing to take on this new challenge?"

Hal and Winnie looked at each other. They knew each other well enough to know they shared a common dream—to take the gospel to people who had never heard it. Hal cleared his throat, "Well, we came at the Lord's leading. Should we stop following His leading now? God has placed before us an open door for the gospel. I think we should walk through it." Winnie smiled and reached over to take his hand in her own… Yes, they would go.

3

Chapter

Bustle

"When do we leave?" Hal asked, almost breathlessly. Things were happening so fast he almost expected Ed to say they would be leaving tomorrow, and the Fosters had arrived at Port Moresby only today.

But Ed's reply was more sympathetic than that. "As soon as you can get your supplies organized. And you will also have to spend a day at the Council on Primitives office. They will not only want to meet you but give you as much information on the Morobuku people as possible."

Winnie's heart seemed to skip a beat as she heard the name of the tribe they would be working with…hopefully. *My, it certainly sounds primitive enough*, she thought to herself. Aloud, she said, "I hope we can have a few days to get better acquainted with all our new brothers and sisters and nieces and nephews."

Ed laughed, "Yes! I think that's a good idea. You arrived here only this morning. I think you could use some time to prepare for this new challenge. How about two weeks? That way, you can stay as long as the Merchants and Crafts are here."

Winnie relaxed ever so slightly at the prospect of two whole weeks with this loving group. As anxious as she was to help Hal get started on their dreamed-of mission work, she felt genuine relief that it would be postponed a few more days. Decisions had been reached so rapidly there had been no time to think much about what had just occurred, and Winnie could not help the sudden feeling of apprehension that swept over her. Involuntarily she shivered.

"Yes, when the sun goes down, even here in the tropics, we sometimes get a cool breeze. Here, I think I can find you a sweater!" Molly's voice interrupted Winnie's troubled thoughts.

"Oh, no," she laughed. "I'm not really chilled. How could one be chilled here in this tropical atmosphere? I don't think I've ever felt such an oppressive heat as we have experienced today. It's a far cry from Montana!" Everyone in the room laughed at her outburst.

Sally exclaimed, "See my hair? When I first came here it was all the way down to my waist. But the first month we were here it mildewed! I've worn it short ever since."

So many differences, thought Winnie. *I wonder if we can adjust to all of them.*

Sleep came easily for Winnie that night. Hal was surprised at how quickly her breathing became measured and rhythmic. His own mind was full of imaginations. Excitement welled up in him, and he could scarcely force himself to lie still. He did not want his own wakefulness to disturb the rest of his exhausted wife. *Am I insane to bring her to such a place?* his troubled thoughts nagged him. For nearly two hours, he leaped from excitement to fear, and back again repeatedly, until the exhaustion of their amazing day finally took its toll, and his breathing came long and deep.

The raucous cries of a crow intruded Hal's dream. He saw himself on the high plains of eastern Montana with a scorching August sun beating down upon him while the crow cawed from a cottonwood branch. But it was not a crow. As Hal began to wake from sleep, he opened his eyes to see a brightly hued parrot on a branch outside the window of their bedroom. *Not much different from the cry of a crow or a blue jay*, Hal thought to himself. A fly walked down the side of his face, and he reached up to brush it away. But when his hand reached his face, he realized it was a bead of perspiration trickling down beside his ear. It was not really a fly at all.

It was early morning, but already the heat was stifling. "We will just have to get used to it," Hal reasoned. He reached for his tee shirt and used it like a towel, wiping the perspiration from his chest. Looking over at Winnie, still asleep, he noticed how a moist brown curl stuck to the side of her face.

Work on preparations began immediately after breakfast. Because they were not going into the bush this trip, Ed and Mary began helping Hal and Winnie sort the supplies they would need to take to Morobuku Island.

One by one the crates were opened, and their contents spread on the floor. Things to take were placed on one side of the room, things to leave behind were put back into the crates and stacked on the other side of the room. After half a day's work, Winnie realized they would be leaving more than they would be taking. "They'll have to fly you there in a small floatplane," Ed explained. "You will be camping out at first. As you need these things, we will send more of your items with the later supply trips."

Indeed, many of the items being prepared for the adventure reminded Winnie of the times she and Hal had prepared for camping in the Rockies. There were sleeping bags, a tent, a portable camp stove (they would have to go into town to get an adequate supply of fuel for the stove prior to leaving), dried foods, medical supplies, a plastic tarpaulin (bright yellow); except for the books and writing materials, the pile of provisions looked very much like they were preparing to load up the Jeep for a jaunt into the mountains for a camping vacation.

The sorting process and the filling in of the necessary things purchased in Port Moresby took actually more than a week. The business of preparation, and the Bible studies and swapping of experiences among the natives by the veteran missionaries made the time pass quickly. When the day arrived for their appointment at the Council on Primitives office, Hal and Winnie had scarcely time to become nervous.

The lettering on the sign by the doorway read, "Council on Primitives—Major Thornton Billup, General Secretary." This office was under the authority of Royal Papua New Guinea Constabulary.

Hal was grateful for Ed's presence as they entered the building. Glass cases in the foyer contained many articles of clothing, tools, and weapons used by various native cultures found in those South Pacific regions. Photographs and paintings on the walls depicted lifestyles Hal had only seen in books and in the pages of National Geographic.

Major Billup was a pleasant surprise. He was slightly past middle age, and his once muscular build had softened into paunchiness. The baldness at the crown of his head was surrounded by the salt-and-pepper fringe of a man in his late fifties or early sixties. He was jovial as introductions were made, but his expression quickly changed to one of careful concern as he approached the subject of the Morobuku people.

"We are willing to allow you to go to the Morobukuni only because of the record of cooperation established by the Harts and their coworkers," Major Billup began. "We will be very adamant in our insistence that these people's culture be disturbed as little as possible. On the other hand, we fear that they may well be discovered soon anyway, and we would rather their first in-depth encounters with civilized man be a good experience, and not a bad one. Heaven knows, there are enough people out there who would try to exploit them if they knew of their existence!" He spoke with an accent, and Hal leaned forward in his chair in an effort to understand every phrase.

"You won't be in much danger," the major continued. "These natives are shy, but not fearful to the point of being dangerous. They are not warlike because they have had no enemies. There are no other tribal groups on the island, just the Morobuku people."

"Physically, the Morobukuni resemble the Maori of New Zealand rather than the negroid Papuans. They are smaller than the average American or Australian. We have had some limited contact with them when we have sent survey teams to Morobuku, and they have seemed friendly enough on those occasions. Of course, we don't know their language. We use sign language to communicate with them."

"When do we leave?" asked Hal.

"Day after tomorrow, if you can be ready by then," Billup replied then smiled, "Do you think you are ready for such a challenge?"

"With God's help, we will be," Hal spoke softly but firmly.

But then, Ed spoke up. "Could we put that off for a month? Hal and Winifred have never been around primitive people. If you would allow us some time, I think it would be wise for the Fosters to spend at least of couple of weeks with the tribal people we are already working with."

Major Billup replied, "I can only give you three weeks. We just can't put this situation off any longer. But Godspeed to you," Billup exclaimed, extending his hand, first to Hal, then to Winnie, and finally to Ed.

4
Chapter

Papuan Natives

When Hal, Winnie, and Ed returned to their headquarters, they had already decided that Hal and Winnie should go to the place where the Merchant family worked with the Mika tribe. But Bob and Sally Merchant were to have a few more days before they returned to their work, and then they would have a full day's journey to get to their destination. There would not be enough room in their four-wheel-drive vehicle with all the supplies they needed for Hal and Winnie to accompany them. If Ed could arrange an airplane to take Hal and Winnie to that location where the Merchants were doing their ministry, that might work. They would have to ask Bob about that.

Later that evening, all four families met to decide exactly what to do with this new opportunity. Bob and Sally were willing to have the Fosters come to be with them for two weeks in order for Hal and Winnie to spend some time with the Mika people. There would not be much time for the Fosters to get acquainted with these Stone Age people, but it would at least give them some idea of how to treat them and how these people would respond to them.

There had been an airstrip made in that mountainous region, so the Fosters could be shuttled in and out of that valley, and the

Merchants had enough room in their home, so Hal and Winnie could stay with them. The most important thing was how Hal and Winnie would get along with the Mika people. This opportunity would give them a chance to understand these natives.

The Fosters had worked with Native American Indians in Montana, but American Indians are no longer primitive. Some of the older Indians still hold to some of the old ways, but the young are just like any other American kids. They dress just like all the other youth at school, and their habits are the same as all the other non-native youths. Most native Americans are exactly like non-native Americans.

But this will be a different situation for the Fosters. They will be meeting, for the first time, actual Stone Age people, people who live like their ancestors lived. Civilization had not yet turned the Mika people into modern people. They still held to the old ways, their old taboos, and superstitions. That is why these missionaries had come to them, to teach them of a Savior who gave His life for them, even for these Stone Age people. But these particular missionaries did not try to change the Mika lifestyle, except to rid their fear of demons, evil spirits, and superstitions and share with them the God who loves them.

For a few more days, the Merchants, the Crafts, and the Harts shared much information with Hal and Winnie about the natives they had worked with—how to treat them and how to respond to them. These natives have eternal souls just like modern civilized people have. They have minds that can think, reason, and imagine. Their minds are able to understand just as any modern person thinks. It is just that they have been in a Stone Age atmosphere for all their lives and know nothing of the outside world.

When the time came for the Merchants to leave, the Fosters had some more sorting and packing to do. First, for their two weeks with the Merchants and with the Mika people, and then to be ready for their journey to the Morobuku Island. What a journey the Fosters had come to, totally different from any other experience in their entire lives! But they wanted to share the Lord's hope to people who had no hope.

Ed had arranged for a bush pilot to take the Fosters to the airstrip near the Merchants' ministry, and also after two weeks, to go there again to return them to Port Moresby. Soon the Fosters were in the air over a thick jungle and over mountains completely covered with jungle growth. They had never seen anything like that before. In Montana, there were clearings in valleys and some mountains rising above the tree line but not here in New Guinea. It was jungle, jungle, jungle.

As their plane went down into a hollow between mountains, Hal noticed the airstrip. It was a very frightening sight. There was barely room for the plane to land and then to take off again. Thankfully, these pilots knew how to do that…most of the time. There had been a few times when these planes crashed, and usually their passengers were victims of that crash… But this time, the pilot did his job. He was experienced. Hal and Winnie had made their destination to the Mika Valley, and there were Bob and Sally Merchant and young Barry to meet them.

There were also nearly naked natives in the group, desiring to see these new strangers who had come to see and meet them. The men had knives tucked into their waistband that held their coverings over their private areas. The few women who were curious enough to see these new strangers had short skirts made of palm thatch or grass that covered them nearly down to their knees. Of course, all these Mika people were curious about these new visitors, but only a few came to see them. These people were afraid of meeting total strangers. They had in their history many wars with other nearby native tribes. It would take some time for these natives to completely trust these new visitors.

The Merchant family guided Hal and Winnie to their home, but not before some of the natives reached out and touched the Fosters to see if these white skins were just like their dark skins. Were these white-skinned people actually real people? They were shorter than the other white-skinned people who had come to live with them. And why are they here among us? Hal and Winnie allowed these Mika people to touch them. They wanted these people to trust them, even the short time they would be with them.

Later, Hal would go out with Bob to meet some of the Mika men. Some of these men had boar tusks or bones pierced through their noses. These were signs that these men had killed a boar or some other animal. That was their badge of authenticity that they were true hunters and warriors. Most of the men had fringes of fur around their arms like arm bands. That was also an indication that they were hunters and warriors. Hal reached out to these men, as at first they may have distrusted him, but the more Hal was with these men, the men relaxed and realized that Hal was a lot like Bob. Of course, Barry was with his dad when Bob took Hal out to meet these Mika men, and those men really liked Barry. That helped smooth the feelings of these men with Hal.

During the two weeks that Hal and Winnie were with the Merchants and with the Mika people, the Fosters learned much about how to interact with these primitive people. They knew only a few of the words that the Merchants had shared with them, words like "*Thank you,*" "*Hello,*" "*Friends,*" and the like. But the Fosters were beginning to hear Mika words that would help them learn to hear and understand what the Morobuku people would be speaking. Of course, it would be a totally different language, with different accents and different sounds, but these two weeks among the Mika people would prepare the Fosters for the people they would meet on the Morobuku Island.

Sally also took Winnie out to meet with the women. These women, wearing these frond skirts, were bare from the waist up. In a native culture like this, women are extremely second-class members of the tribe. Their work is to bear children and do the cooking and gardening. Some of them are treated well by their husbands, but most are not. They are just beasts of burden to their husbands. But the husbands who have allowed Jesus to come into their lives have become more tolerant and more loving toward their women.

The native women of Papua New Guinea live in fear most of the time. Their husbands may beat them if they don't do everything just the right way. Also, when they go out to collect the taro roots in the garden or to till the garden, they have to be aware that an enemy warrior may be lurking nearby to shoot arrows into them. Some of the tribes still practice cannibalism.

Winnie also reached out to these women when Sally brought her to them. And they reached out to Winnie. They wanted to see another white woman like Sally. It was so strange for them to see these white women wearing such strange coverings over their bodies. They also wanted to see if these white women were strong enough to till a garden or to butcher a hog. Some of them grasped Winnie's arms to see if she actually had strength in her muscles. But most of them were pleased with Winnie's reactions to them.

The Merchants introduced Hal and Winnie to the foods the natives survived on. The taro roots, similar to sweet potatoes, and the wild pig meat, and the wild fruits that could be gathered in the jungle. Sally taught Winnie how to prepare these foods, but of course, they also had normal civilized foods to prepare for their meals. Hal and Winnie learned so much from the Merchants during the two weeks they spent with them, and also, how to react and mingle with the natives.

The first night Hal and Winnie were in the bedroom in the Merchants' home, they talked about how they had met and mingled with the Mika people. They shared the different experiences they had with the natives. But then Winnie shuddered. "I hope I can get used to the smell of these people. They smell so horribly. They have pig fat on their bodies and don't keep themselves clean. I want to learn to love these people, and I want to accept their way of living. I surely hope I can do that."

The two weeks the Fosters stayed with the Merchants really helped them to understand what they were going to have to endure when going to the Morobukuni people. These two weeks really strengthened their resolve to love the people they were going to, people they had very little knowledge of.

During the evenings at the Merchants' home, Bob and Sally began teaching Hal and Winnie some of the sign language they would need to communicate with the people they were going to. Since they would not know the language, there was sign language that many tribes used so they could communicate with each other if they did not know the other people's language. This should be a great help to the Fosters.

When the Fosters got into the plane to go back to Port Moresby and the Harts' home, Hal was thinking, *Can this pilot get this plane airborne out of this jungle? Is the runway long enough?* But the pilot did his job. He had done so many times. He was experienced and knew exactly what to do.

5
Chapter

Morobuku

Before they could leave the Council on Primitives office, the Fosters and Ed Hart were required to spend some time with the undersecretary and two of his aides. They were briefed on the island climate, plant and animal life, and some of the tribal customs of the Morobuku that were known. The Morobuku were not warlike but practiced communal living, not for protection but to make accomplishment of tasks simpler.

"You should be at the domestic airport terminal at 7:00 AM, Friday. We will fly you to Bougainville on a commercial flight, where you will disembark by way of a shuttle bus to the seaplane dock. Mr. Jamison will accompany you to Bougainville and see that you get your gear and supplies transferred to the floatplane. From there, it will just be the two of you and your pilot." The undersecretary was not as jovial as Major Billup had been, but he was cordial enough in his businesslike manner.

Mr. Jamison was young. He had a slow smile that matched the slowness of his thick New Guinea accent. Tousled brown hair above a tanned complexion suggested that he was an active outdoor type. No doubt he cherished the idea of accompanying the Fosters to Bougainville. It would get him out of the office for a day.

It was early afternoon when they left the government offices to return to Ed and Mary's house. The house seemed empty with the seven people and several months of the missionary supplies gone.

Mary had prepared a lunch for the tired trio, and she began setting it on the kitchen table when they came in the door. "I didn't know how long you would be gone, so I just prepared sandwiches," Mary said.

"Sandwiches are fine. I could eat a horse!" Ed exclaimed.

Mary's humorous reply was, "Don't be too sure you're not!" All four of the missionaries laughed, the two veterans and the two raw recruits.

The time had passed all too quickly. Hal and Winnie's belongings had been pared down to the bare necessities. All the supplies had been bundled in heavy plastic to shield them from the tropical rains they would surely encounter. Food stuffs had been stored in resealable tins to protect them from any marauding animals that might otherwise make themselves unwelcome guests.

Plus some basic medical supplies also went with their packs. Both Hal and Winnie had taken a few classes on medical situations they might face, for themselves and also for the people they were trying to reach. Fortunately, Winnie had been studying to become a nurse, but the rapidity of their going to linguistics training detained her from finishing the course to get her certificate. But the training had done well for her, and she knew much about physical health situations.

The half-hour trip in the minibus to the airport terminal was not at all uncomfortable. There was plenty of room in the van for the four people and the meager supplies and camping gear that would provide survival for the Fosters for the next weeks and months.

"I remember one time when I was supposed to fly to the mouth of the Fly River at Daru and take a boat upstream to contact the Biakami tribe right up by the West Irian border," Ed reminisced. "I almost missed my plane because I went to the international terminal instead of the domestic terminal."

It was hard for the Fosters to see Ed and Mary leave.

The single engine plane droned on. It had taken four hours to get to Bougainville from Port Moresby, about six hundred miles in a turboprop twin-engine plane, and now the going was even slower. They had taken time to eat lunch at Bougainville and get last-minute instructions from Jamison. The floatplane would bring more supplies and check on them at Morobuku after one week. After then, the supply trips would be one month apart.

"We want to monitor your progress," Jamison said, "as well as to help you keep in touch with the outside world." Winnie was glad for that news.

Two hours out from Bougainville, Harold Gray, the pilot, reached over and tapped Hal on the knee. He pointed to a green dot on the horizon. "There it is," he spoke loudly over the engine noise. "Morobuku."

Hal squinted, and Winnie leaned forward from her seat behind him to look at the green speck as it began to grow larger and take shape before their eyes. The closer they drew, the greener the island became. At a distance, it had appeared to be very dark, but as they drew nearer, it took on emerald hues. Mountains took form, covered with thick jungle growth all the way to the tops, some of which had sheer cliffs on their western slopes.

As they approached, the pilot appeared to be diving toward the side of the mountain itself until Hal noticed a gap in the wall of green before them. Beneath them, an aquamarine ribbon grew to a fiord-like bay, knifing its way back between the vertical cliffs. As their craft descended into the maw of the abyss, the beauty of the scene nearly took their breath away. The floats touched the surface of the bay and glided to a stop on the edge of a narrow sandbar beach. All three were silent as they drank in the scene with their eyes. It was as if they had invaded the sanctuary of Eden itself.

Suddenly, Hal reacted. He opened the door with a jerk, and with a bound to the float that made the small plane shudder, and with another leap, he was on the sand. Stooping down he scooped a handful of sand and let it trickle through his fingers as he assessed the beauty with his eyes and nostrils. Fragrant blossoms wafted their scent on the moist air currents. Caught up for a reverent moment in the pristine surroundings, Hal almost forgot there was anyone else around.

"Well, are you just going to stand there, or are you going to help me down?" Winnie called from the cabin of the plane. "I think Mr. Gray wants to get back to Bougainville before dark!" Hal awoke from his trance and went to help Winnie down to the beach.

"Kind of takes your breath away, doesn't it?" Harold Gray remarked. "I was here last week when those COP people came to look the area over. There's a clear stream that empties into the bay just up there about a quarter of a kilometer," he waved toward the end of the bay.

Hal could see a waterfall through the banana trees and guessed it must be the stream Gray indicated.

"That grassy knoll up there will be a good place for your base camp. You'll be able to see in any direction for a couple hundred yards, and you can see me coming from there when I fly back in."

Moments later, the baggage was all on the beach, and the engine of the floatplane was revving up. "Be back one week from today," Gray shouted out the open door before closing it tightly. Then the little plane taxied away on its water runway, and gaining speed, lifted from the surface in a spray of diamonds in the afternoon sun.

Hal and Winnie watched until the plane disappeared around the curve of volcanic cliffs guarding the bay. For a brief moment they heard the drone of the plane's engine…then silence. They stood alone on the edge of paradise: Morobuku.

6
Chapter

Home

"It's already midafternoon," Hal said. "If we're going to get camp set up by nightfall, we'd better start carrying this gear up the hill." Beginning to work while he spoke, Hal picked up the heaviest bundle first. Indicating a much lighter one for Winnie to carry, he said, "You take that one, then you can start opening these at the camp site while I carry the rest of our bundles up the hill."

Winnie did not want to take her eyes from the place on the mountain around which the floatplane had disappeared. A momentary wave of fear swept over her, but she shrugged it aside and turned to the task at hand. Gathering the lighter bundle indicated by Hal, she followed him up the slope.

There was not a trail, but the undergrowth was not too thick, and the climb to the campsite was not difficult. At the top of the knoll was a cluster of small trees with foliage spread out like a canopy. The lower branches were at least five feet above Hal's head as he stood beneath them. They would later learn that these trees were referred to as *umbrella trees* in the tropics, and it was a good name for them. The branches and leaves formed a natural shelter from the heat of a midday sun.

"This large bundle has our tent, stove, and cooking utensils in it. I'll untie it for you, and you can unpack it while I go for another load." Winnie did as Hal suggested, thankful for his energetic efficiency. This was not the first time they had camped together. An hour and several trips later, Hal had carried every package from the beach to the hilltop, and Winnie had set up the nylon cabin tent and erected the stove on its stand beneath a yellow nylon kitchen fly. The tree trunks and limbs had proven to be handy places to tie the guy lines for the kitchen fly.

Hal found the folding aluminum table and set it up. Three folding chairs were placed beside the table. "What's the third chair for?" asked Winnie.

"We want to be ready for our island visitors at all times, don't we?" he replied. Winnie smiled at his optimistic cheeriness.

Supper was made from canned goods they had brought with them, and they sat in their folding chairs at their folding table and enjoyed the rustle of a gentle breeze in nature's green canopy above them. The quiet peacefulness of the setting surrounded them, and for a short while, they were oblivious to the newness and strangeness of their surroundings. There seemed to be no danger in the world at all.

"Look at it: Morobuku Bay," Winnie breathed.

"Morobuku Bay?" Hal asked, his eyebrows raised.

"Sure. Can you think of a better name for it?"

"I don't believe I can," he surrendered to her thought. "Morobuku Bay it shall be!"

Hal went to one of the plastic-wrapped bundles and returned with his Bible. "It's time we thank and praise the Lord for bringing us here." He opened the book to Psalm 91. "He who dwells in the shelter of the Most High will abide in the shadow of the Almighty. I will say to the Lord, 'My refuge and my fortress, My God, in whom I trust!'"

He read on, "He will cover you with His pinions and under His wings you may seek refuge... You will not be afraid of the terror by night, or of the arrow that flies by day... No evil will befall you, nor will any plague come near your tent."

Winnie relaxed even more as he read. *How wonderful!* she thought. *We have no reason to fear because God is our refuge and fortress.* She noticed that darkness was beginning to fall. "No fear of the terror by night," she sighed thankfully.

Sleep claimed them both within minutes after they retired. A gentle sea breeze passed through the screened windows of the tent. They had no way of knowing how long they had slept when they were shocked to wakefulness by horrifying screams from the nearby jungle.

"What's that, Hal?" Winnie's heart was racing wildly as fear rose up into her throat. She had to stifle a scream of her own.

Hal was startled, too, and had leaped from the air mattress bed on the floor of the tent. He was standing at the window facing the edge of the forest, but it was too dark to see anything. The chilling screams were repeated, only this time farther away. Then, after an interval of a few minutes, yet farther away.

"I don't know what it is," spoke Hal finally. "It may be monkeys. There are supposed to be some on the island. South America has monkeys called *howlers.* Maybe this is something like that."

"Are you afraid?" Winnie asked with a quiver in her voice.

"No, I'm not afraid."

"Then what are you doing with that machete in your hand?"

Hal laughed. "I guess maybe I was a little bit scared. That sure was a horrible sound!" With that, he unzipped the screen door and stepped outside, still clutching the machete in his hand.

After several minutes he called, "Winnie, come out here!"

"What's the matter?" she replied, not at all certain she wanted to leave the dubious safety of the tent.

"The stars," he explained. "They're very bright tonight." Winnie came and stood by his side, and he put his arm around her, part in protection, but more in affection.

"Look up there! Do you see it?"

"See what?" she replied, trying in the darkness to see what he was indicating by pointing with his other outstretched arm.

"The Southern Cross. It's our first night alone beneath the Southern Cross." She recognized the constellation Sid Craft had pointed out to them during their stay at Port Moresby. She shivered slightly and snuggled closer to her protector.

"We don't have anything to fear, you know," Hal said later when they were once again lying on their bed. "There's not supposed to be any dangerous animals here, and we do want to contact the Morobukuni, don't we?" He continued, "And don't you remember the Scripture passage we read this evening? 'No evil will befall you, nor will any plague come near your tent.'"

The twitter of small birds and rays of sunshine combined to waken the sleepers. They both arose and got dressed and began preparing breakfast. Hal set to work getting more of their bundles opened to have the items they would need for the next few days readily at hand.

"What's on the agenda for today?" Winnie asked over a second cup of tea. "Water," Hal replied. "We have to find a good source of clean water to drink and cook with."

"There's the stream right there," Winnie gestured toward the swift torrent tumbling over the boulders on its final steep descent to Morobuku Bay.

"I'm afraid we might have dysentery if we used that water without boiling it first. What I want to find is the source of a spring coming out of the ground. If I can find the water at its source, it should be pure."

Winnie cleaned up the breakfast dishes and hung their food supply from a rope stretched high between two trees, a trick Hal had learned while camping in bear country in Montana. Hal gathered the things he would need for his little exploring expedition: a machete, a length of rope, a canvas water bag, and a small camera. He gave the rope and camera to his wife as they prepared to hike out of camp. Winnie placed the coil of rope over her head and placed one arm and shoulder through it. "There! I'll bet we look just like Stanley and Livingstone setting out into deepest Africa," she joked.

"Maybe more like Laurel and Hardy," Hal teased, and she gave him a playful shove.

Their route took them from the grassy knoll where they had camped, up to a level plateau scattered with trees. Thick groves of bamboo lined the banks of the stream, which had slowed its rushing to match the more level terrain. The open plateau may have covered nearly a square mile before it became hidden by thick jungle. A short distance beyond that, the mountains narrowed to a steep gorge from which direction the stream flowed.

Coming to a small brook one could jump across in some places, they followed it up the side of the mountain where it bubbled up from rocky gravel at the base of a cliff. This was what Hal had been looking for. "I think we should build our house near here," Hal spoke with a hint of excitement in his voice. "Right over there, on that little rise above the rocky outcropping. It will give us a good view in every direction except the mountain behind it. We can see the bay from there and virtually all of the open plateau."

"How will they get our building supplies to us?" Winnie asked.

"It's already here," Hal answered patiently. "We have lots of bamboo and palm and banana leaf thatch to build our house with. We're going to be real pioneers."

"Then we're home!" Winnie exclaimed, and she felt the tingle of a thrill surge through her.

7
Chapter

Grandview

The decision to build a bamboo house on the plateau immediately prompted another decision. The camp would need to be moved from beneath the umbrella trees to a site adjacent to the proposed bamboo house. Having made that decision, the rest of the morning was spent tearing down the original camp and relocating the supplies to the plateau site. Midday found them moved and ready to set up camp again.

"I think we should call this place Grandview," announced Winnie over a hastily prepared lunch of canned meat, dried fruit, and Tang made with cool spring water.

"You seem to have a yen for naming things," Hal said. "Are you sure your name isn't Mrs. Adam?"

Grandview was a good site for a house. Digging a hole for a refuse pit, Hal discovered the top of the rock that came out just below the rise in an outcropping. It was four feet down from the surface of the soil. *Just the perfect depth for the posts to be planted to serve as a foundation for our house. It will literally be built on solid rock!* Hal thought.

With the aid of some strategically placed bamboo poles Hal cut from the stream bank, the kitchen fly was erected, the tent set up, and an orderly and efficient camp established. That project accomplished by midafternoon, Hal took his bow saw and machete and went to the bamboo thickets to begin collecting building materials for the house. The Crafts had told Hal that there are different varieties of bamboo. To set the poles for the house, Hal would have to look for large diameter bamboo with a small center hole in the middle. These would be the strongest bamboo poles to support the house he would build. And it took Hal some time to find the bamboo he needed. He spent more than an hour to find the thicket that had thicker and sturdier poles of bamboo, but by looking for the larger bamboo, he finally discovered some that should work for the foundation poles for their house.

In the meantime, Winnie worked with the portable stove and folding table and two of the packing crates to organize her *kitchen*. She scraped away the vegetation from a large circular area and arranged some stones to form a firepit. "Done as well as Hal could have done it," she said smugly to herself. Much of the cooking done on their camping trips in Montana had been accomplished over an open fire.

On one of his trips to the site with a load of bamboo poles, Hal noticed with satisfaction the progress Winnie was making on her kitchen. On another trip, Hal saw that she had stretched two braided net hammocks between tree trunks near the tent. "That will be cooler sleeping, that's for sure," he called to her.

Late in the afternoon, when Hal had decided that his tired arms did not want to cut any more bamboo, he gathered the butt ends of two of the largest bamboo poles under his arms and trudged toward camp, dragging the long poles behind him travois style. When he drew near the campsite, his nostrils detected a familiar, yet unexpected scent. It smelled like fish frying.

Winnie looked up and saw her husband approaching. "Supper's almost ready," she called to him.

"Where did you get the fish?" Hal asked incredulously.

"Where do you always get fresh fish? From the water, silly," Winnie responded saucily. "While you were pretending to be a lumberjack, I went fishing. You see, I remember some of what you taught me about the out-of-doors." Hal grinned at her.

Later, Winnie admitted that the fish were not at all spooked by her presence on the stream bank. The water was so clear they couldn't help but notice her yet showed no fear. They competed for her worm baited hook with reckless abandon. The freshwater fish from the stream would prove to be a very welcome addition to their diet during their stay at the Grandview site.

Their second evening on Morobuku was spent swinging lazily in their hammocks, singing gospel choruses together and gazing out over the grassy plateau in the evening sunlight. The peace was heightened by the soft light of the lowering sun. A soft breeze brushed lightly over the grassy plain. The leaves of the few trees clustered around the knoll whispered their satisfaction at the caressing of the gently moving salt air.

Winnie glanced over at her husband, him having fallen silent. His breathing betrayed the fact that the labors of the day had taken their toll. The rhythmic rocking of the hammock had lulled him to sleep.

Later, in their temporary tent home, both tired young missionaries slept a peaceful sleep. This night, they were not interrupted by the loud cries of their first night's stay. The rest they gained was much needed and replenished their supply of energy for tomorrow's work.

Sunday morning's light revealed an overcast sky. A light rain pattered on the tent roof for an hour after daylight came, then gradually diminished until the rain stopped completely and rays of sunlight began to pierce the widening gaps between the clouds.

Hal had planned no work for that day, it being set aside for worship and reflection on God's great goodness. He helped Winnie with breakfast, and afterward, they read to each other from the Bible and shared a very private and holy communion service. The balance of the morning was spent discussing the spiritual principles that had been shared among the more experienced missionaries during their stay at Port Moresby, and also their experiences with the Mika people that the Merchants were working with.

In God's eyes, there is no difference between the primitive aborigine and the most sophisticated civilized man, except that the primitive man may be more beloved because he more readily accepts the gospel with childlike faith. Jesus had said, "Unless you are converted and become like children, you shall not enter the kingdom of heaven." He had also said, "Blessed are the poor in spirit, for theirs is the kingdom of heaven."

Winnie had reflected on her own feelings of prejudice and attitudes of superiority that had troubled her when she and Hal had worked together at summer camps and Bible schools for reservation Indians in Montana and Wyoming. Would she be able to put those attitudes of prideful superiority behind her when they might finally have the opportunity to work among the Morobukuni people?

Following a light lunch, Hal and Winnie searched for a way to cross the stream. A few hundred yards upstream, they discovered a shallow riffle where the stream widened to run over a smooth bed of gravel. They removed their shoes and waded across calf deep in the cool water.

They explored the small open plain on the other side of the stream for most of the afternoon, discovering many luxuriant and beautiful plants and smelling the sweetness of frangipani at several different locations, the small pixie-bonnet blossoms casting their fragrance carelessly about. The plain was dotted with clusters of trees: a grove of coconut palms here, a bunch of banana trees there, and several other types of trees these North Americans could not identify.

The hike was a pleasant one, but in the heat of the afternoon, wading the stream at the riffle to return to their home on Grandview was quite refreshing. The orange tent and yellow nylon kitchen fly were visible for a great distance, and during their walk, the sight of it in the distance had given Winnie a warm feeling of security. *Isn't it strange how we attach feelings of security to material things that can be swept away in a moment?* she thought, yet she did not voice that thought aloud.

The early days of the week were used up in Hal's gathering of bamboo poles and palm branches for the construction of their house. Much of Winnie's time was spent trying to plan ways in which to make a variety of meals out of their dwindling supply of dried and canned foods.

Hal began to construct the framework of their house. First, he dug holes down through the soil to the solid rock beneath. The first two post holes were excavated with the small folding spade he had included in his camping supplies, but the labor was too slow to suit him. Then he devised a remarkably effective post-hole digger from the largest piece of bamboo he had harvested from the streamside groves.

He sharpened one end of the bamboo at an angle, then cut a slot in it up to the solid joint until he had fashioned a tool that looked much like a very oversize apple corer. When he punched and twisted the piece of bamboo into the soil, then pulled it out, it removed the soil in the core of the bamboo and left a smooth sided hole in the ground as a result. Hal's project progressed at a much more rapid pace after the invention and use of the bamboo post-hole digger.

Girders for a raised floor about five feet off the ground added stability to the structure after all the poles had been set and tamped securely into their respective post holes. The floor girders and then roof rafters were tied into place with tough nylon cord Bob Merchant had the foresight to recommend to be included in their first load of supplies.

On Friday, Hal was just lashing one of the rafters to the ridge pole when he thought he heard a low humming sound. A few moments later, he knew he had not been mistaken, for around the curve of the cliffs above Morobuku Bay he saw the white wings of the floatplane reflected in the midmorning sun.

It would be good for both of them to see another human face.

8
Chapter

Noah

Harold Gray had noticed the colorful tent and kitchen fly as he lowered his floatplane into the canyon that walled in Morobuku Bay. "They've moved their camp," he said to himself as he set the floats on the water and coasted to the sandy beach. In the week that had passed since he had left the personable young couple on Morobuku, he had thought of them often, wondering how they would fare on what seemed to him to be a risky assignment.

He was not an employee of the Papua New Guinea government. His private seaplane charter service had been contracted to haul supplies and keep in contact with these brave young missionaries. He was well acquainted with most of the islands within a day's flight of Bougainville, but he had been taken entirely by surprise when the Council on Primitives had revealed to him a map showing the location of Morobuku. He had not known such an island existed. Few people did.

The propeller of the single engine craft was decreasing in revolutions and nearly still as the pilot stepped from the cabin to the plane's float. He had seen the Fosters hurrying down the path they had beaten into the grass a week earlier when they had carried their belongings up the hill. By the time Gray stepped on the sandy beach, the Fosters were there too.

"Hello! How's the bushmen?" he said as he reached out to accept Hal's offered handshake. "I wondered how you'd do. Did you make contact with the natives yet?"

Hal replied, "No, we haven't seen anything of them. But we did hear something our first night here. Something screamed in the middle of the night and woke us up. It kept screaming at intervals, but it kept getting farther away."

"Oh, a screamer, no doubt! It's a little gray bird no bigger than your fist, but it surely can make a loud sound," the pilot answered. Hal and Winnie both laughed to think the thing that had so frightened them their first night on Morobuku had only been a little gray bird.

"Well, are you ready to go back to civilization, or shall we unload your supplies?"

"We're here to stay!" Hal responded, and stepped toward the plane to begin the unloading. In a short time, all the parcels were on the beach, wrapped in heavy, watertight plastic as before.

"Thought I'd come early in the day and stay a few hours before heading back," Gray said. "I'll help you get your gear up to your camp."

The two men began the task of carrying the supplies the quarter mile to Grandview. "Why don't we carry the stuff as far as the original camp site until we get all of it off the beach, then carry them the rest of the distance later?" Hal suggested, so they carried their loads the first two hundred yards and deposited them there until all the bundles were ready to be carried the final distance to their home site.

Most of the packages were too heavy for Winnie, so she took a lighter one she could manage and went on ahead to Grandview. She was grateful for Gray's company, if just for a few hours. She hadn't realized how lonely she had felt until she saw the man step from the plane. She knew that one of the greatest trials she and Hal would face would be the isolation from other people with whom they could converse. She hoped the day was not too far off when they would encounter their hoped-for Morobuku people.

"I see you've begun a house," she heard Gray speak as the two men approached the new campsite with the first burdens of their portage. "If you're not familiar with building with bamboo, I'd be happy to show you a few tricks," Gray continued.

"Oh, please do," spoke Hal quickly. "I'm just doing the best I can, but I know there have to be better ways to do it than the way I've been doing it."

When the final portage had been made, the two men rested for a few minutes, talking about Hal's bamboo house project. "If you split your bamboo down the middle, end to end, you can overlap the two halves and make a wall. By placing the edge of one bamboo into the hollow of the next, you will keep out most of the weather. They sent you some galvanized wire from the mainland on this load. You can use it to fasten those joints stronger than if you use only nylon rope. I brought more of that, too," he added.

The hours passed much too quickly with the helpful floatplane pilot. As the Fosters stood on the sandy beach watching the plane climb into the sky, Winnie felt a lump rise in her throat. She was near tears when she was suddenly stung by flying sand. She turned and saw Hal grinning mischievously. She ran at him, and they wrestled playfully until they both fell into the warm ripples of Morobuku Bay. Laughing and giggling, they stood and walked out of the water and began the climb to their home in paradise, sand from the beach sticking to their wet shoes and clothing.

Later, they sorted their supplies and stored them on the shoulder-high bamboo platform Hal had constructed to use as a cache until their house was completed. A heavy plastic sheet, tied down at the corners, protected the cache from the rain and morning dew.

It took nearly two weeks for the completion of the bamboo house. Hal followed Harold Gray's suggestion and constructed panels of split bamboo for the walls. More split bamboo was used in laying a floor over the bamboo girders.

After laying the floor for the living-dining area, which was already five feet off the ground, Hal decided it would be well to raise the floor level for the bedroom a little higher to get as much tropical breeze as possible to help cool their warm nights. There would be no really cool seasons. They were located four degrees south of the equator. There were only wet and dry seasons. This was the dry season.

Hal tied the floor joists for the bedroom securely to the notched posts three feet higher than the floor of the living area. The larger bamboo he had cut were well over twenty feet long and six inches in diameter, so his making the bedroom floor a few feet higher would not diminish the strength of the structure. The result of the raised room was a split-level two-room house with a ground-level area beneath the bedroom to be utilized as an additional room at some future time.

Another of Harold Gray's ideas was to construct the bamboo walls with large windows halfway up from the floor. The window openings extended nearly the entire length of each wall with appropriate braces spaced so as to give some rigidity to the structure. Shutters were constructed for the windows that were tied with nylon cord to hinge at the top. The shutters could be left open most of the time to permit the breezes to flow freely through the house but could be lowered in inclement weather.

The last part of the superstructure to be built was the roof. Hal had placed a stout ridge pole near the top of his two longest posts, about twenty feet above the ground. He had done so prior to his decision to raise the bedroom floor eight feet off the ground, but even with the added wall height, he reasoned that the pitch of the roof would be adequate to repel the rains. After all, in alpine countries, steep roofs were designed to let heavy snow slide off. This roof would only have to repel water that could never collect there to create an overload of weight.

While Hal had been constructing the framework and walls of the house, Winnie had spent her times in between meal preparation holding poles in place while Hal securely lashed them and gathering palm branches for the roof. She was a diligent worker and had accumulated quite a large "haystack" of the branches by the time Hal was ready to put their water-shedding roof on. Her hands and arms had become scratched and rough from the labor, but she knew they would heal quickly when the branch gathering was done.

Finally, the house was complete, and they moved their supplies into it. The tent was folded and suspended beneath the bedroom floor. The air mattresses were placed on the floor until more bamboo could be split to make elevated beds. The few crates they had were utilized in the living-dining area as cabinets and shelves for storage and for Winnie's center of the room, the four folding chairs placed around the perimeter of the room, and they were "home," at home in their own house, made with their own hands, hands that now folded in prayers of thanksgiving.

The rain started during the night. At first, it was a light mist. Then large drops began to hit the palm thatch roof. By morning, it was a full-scale deluge. When they woke, their bedding was already damp from the moist air, or so Winnie thought at first. Then she realized that their new roof was leaking. "Hal," she wailed. "What are we going to do? Everything will be soaked!"

Hal got up quickly, and without getting dressed, he went to their supplies and produced a large plastic sheet. He spread it over the bed and gathered their clothing from the neat stacks Winnie had made of them against one wall and placed the clothing under the plastic. He had noticed water dripping rapidly into the living area also and dashed out into the rain.

"What are you doing?" Winnie called after him.

"I'm going to put up the kitchen fly," he yelled back over his shoulder. True to his word, he came in dragging a long bamboo pole with him. He fastened the pole high up in their "cathedral ceiling" and draped the kitchen fly over it, securing the outer edges of the nylon fabric with nylon ties to the window hinges on either side of the room. The nylon square was not quite as large as the room, but it afforded a moderately dry area in the center of the room. But "dry" could hardly describe the situation. Nearly everything was already wet as a result of the leaking roof.

They sat at their table and looked out over the wet landscape. The rain continued. The stream below was becoming a river. Winnie shivered as she sipped at a cup of hot tea. It was not at all cold, not even cool, but there was no way to escape the dampness.

By late afternoon, the stream was completely out of its banks. The thickets of bamboo which had lined the stream banks were islands in the midst of a moving sea.

Water dripped constantly from the edges of the nylon "ceiling" to the floor, passing on through the cracks between the split bamboo to join the rivulets on their way to swell the volume of the flooded stream. The young couple could do no more than sit and watch.

By nightfall, the river had grown large enough that they could easily hear the roar of the rapids over the sound of the rain as the flood plunged the last one hundred yards steeply to the sea. Morobuku Bay, usually a clear and beautiful blue, had turned a muddy brown, like coffee with cream in it, from the silty floodwaters.

All through the day, the rain had alternated between light mist and heavy downpour, but by evening, it had settled into a moderate but steady rate. It rained on through the night and into the next day, and then another day, and another. By the fourth day, they wondered if it would ever stop. They would have to wait and see.

On the eighth day, Hal said, "I'm beginning to appreciate how Noah must have felt," but there was little humor in his voice. Both young missionaries worked valiantly at keeping their irritability under control. That did not always work for them. They did get irritable. They argued some. They had been in the house for so many days while the rain continued, on and on. To get away from their irritability, they took turns reading to each other from the Bible and from other books they had with them. They took great care to shield all of their paper supplies and books from being dripped on, but they could do nothing about them drawing moisture from the saturated air.

On the ninth day, the rain stopped. The swollen stream continued to be out of its banks for a few days afterward. The rain stopped falling as the clouds began to break up, and then sunlight peeked through. Looking across the meadow on the other side of the stream, Winnie saw a sight that caused her to gasp softly and tug at Hal's arm. A brightly multicolored rainbow arched above the distant jungle.

"Noah's rainbow, I believe," sighed Hal. "A promise of brighter days to come." And it was.

9

Chapter

Visitors

The rain had left its dampness on everything. The days following the rainbow were filled with dragging wet things out of their storage places and spreading them in the sun to dry.

Breaks in the work were spent watching for the various kinds of birds that visited the grassy plain. On occasion, they were able to photograph some of them. Winnie made some quick pencil sketches on her pad of a few of them. Once Hal saw a little gray bird, he thought might be a screamer. Sure enough, the little bird flitted from one tree to another; just as it reached the edge of the thick jungle, it paused on a limb and emitted a shrill scream, not unlike that of a terrified woman.

The day came for the supply plane to arrive. Winnie was anxious to read the letters she had anticipated would arrive with their supplies. News from family fifteen thousand miles away would bring them somewhat closer. She hoped, too, for letters from the churches in Toronto and Billings.

Hal was back in the edge of the thick jungle, gathering more thatch for the roof of the house when Harold Gray's plane arrived in the bay. By the time he could get to the knoll at Grandview and see the plane at the narrow beach, a thoroughly excited Winnie was waving wildly from her position between two men, one of them Harold Gray, the other the unmistakably giant frame of Bob Merchant.

After the handshaking and backslapping were complete, the three men made short work of carrying the fresh supplies to Grandview. Hal and Winnie were eager to hear news Bob would be bringing from their fellow missionaries on the mainland of New Guinea.

"Sally sends her love," Bob said. "She wanted to come along when she discovered my plan to take a couple of extra days and visit you." Bob had brought one of the tribal chiefs to Port Moresby for medical treatment. "Some other time, when we can get away for a few days, I'll bring the whole family for a visit."

Winnie's heart ached within her to think of the possibility of conversation with another woman. How she missed that female companionship she had enjoyed those weeks with Mary, Sally, Molly, and even young Sandie as they prepared for this daring adventure.

"I saw Sid and Molly the other day," Bob was continuing to share the news of the mainland missionary families. "Jamie was not feeling well. He has recurring bouts with the malaria he nearly died from two years ago. Their work with the Amaro people seems to be going well enough, actually, better than ours with the Mika."

Hal listened attentively as the tall man spoke of the work with the New Guinean natives. There were constant problems needing to be solved, not only with the translation work but also in tribal relations. Most of the New Guinea tribes had practiced revenge killing before the missionary influence had nearly put a stop to the violence, and now and again, a fresh conflict would set off fresh killings.

If what the COP people say is true of the Morobukuni, we shouldn't have that kind of trouble here, Hal reassured himself silently.

And there was mail! Winnie read each letter quickly while the men talked, then reread each one more carefully. There was a letter from Molly Craft, a quick, short note from Ed and Mary Hart that Mary had scribbled when she learned that Bob was accompanying the floatplane pilot to the island, and letters from family and friends in America and Canada. *How God's love brings us all together!* Winnie thought as she reveled in her letters.

"Could you put up two tired travelers overnight?" Bob asked.

"Could we ever!" Hal enthused. "We get really lonely here, you know."

Bob laughed, "Yes, I know. Sally and I once spent four months without seeing another civilized face or hearing our language from anyone other than ourselves. We were working with the Kokoma tribe at the time."

During the afternoon, the four of them crossed the stream that was just returning to its normal size after the heavy rains that had soaked the Fosters' belongings. As they walked about the grassy plain, Bob and Harold pointed to edible plants and fruits. Hal and Winnie were already familiar with coconuts and bananas but got some good pointers on when to harvest them. They had seen papayas and mangoes in supermarkets, but not knowing what kind of trees they grew on, they had not recognized them until they were pointed out to them.

"Let me show you how to make baby food," Bob said as he stopped beside a green plant. "This is arrowroot. You dig it like potatoes, boil the roots to get the starch, then use it to make a very digestible baby food or pudding or pie filling. Sally uses this a lot!"

Harold had gone to the edge of the forest by himself while the missionaries were digging the arrowroot out of the ground. "Over here!" he called. "I found something for you over here!" When the group arrived at where Harold was, he had already climbed partway up a tree. He was just dislodging a large green object about the size of a basketball from a springy branch.

"Breadfruit!" he chortled triumphantly. "Nature's variety market. You can prepare this an amazingly different number of ways. You can fry it, bake it, boil it into pudding or paste. And it is even good for you."

Hal took mental notes of all these things, but Winnie was actually writing them down on a sketch pad she had brought along. Beside the name of each food product, she sketched an accurate likeness of the plant from which it came, using her artistic ability to draw the leaves and stems in intricate detail. There were so many kinds of plants in this botanical wonder of a place that she wanted to be certain they harvested only edible produce, not some harmful look-alike that might poison them.

Bob told Winne that Sally had sent along a few recipes on preparing some of this natural produce, and before they returned to Grandview, Winnie made Harold swear solemnly that when he returned the next month with their next load of supplies, he would bring with him not only all of his wife's recipes, but also those of her neighbors.

Supper that evening was a festive occasion for the Fosters. The two experienced South Seas men helped the newcomers prepare their first meal with breadfruit, from main course to dessert. The balance of the evening was spent sharing stories of experiences they all had enjoyed, or endured, depending on the circumstances of each.

Bob roared with laughter when they told him of their fright over the screamer bird, and he nodded in sympathy when they described the soaking they had received in the nine-day rain. "I'll show you what to do about that roof tomorrow morning," he said. "You can thatch it so well that you can go all the way through the three-month rainy season with hardly a drop coming through." *Three months of rain.* Winnie could hardly bear to think about it.

Both Bob and Harold expressed their approval of the clean water supply Hal had discovered at the base of the mountain. Most of what he had done in construction of the house also met with their approval. Hal had been careful to follow Harold's suggestions on fastening the bamboo together.

The next day dawned with the usual tropical delight. Bird songs and flower scents filled the air. Dew on the plants sparkled in the early morning sun. A breakfast of mango and tiny bananas and steaming tea was thoroughly enjoyed by each.

Bob told Hal what he needed to do to increase the water-shedding ability of the thatched roof and made drawings on one of Winnie's sketch pads to ensure that Hal would get it right when he did it. Then the men went out to gather more thatch material. They spent the morning gathering armloads of sun-bleached dry palm branches that were readily available. By increasing the pitch of the roof and the thickness of the thatch Bob promised them a snug and dry house.

By midafternoon, the men had gathered all the palm branches thought necessary to make the needed refinements to the house. What now remained was for Hal, in the days to come, to install the better roof. He would do so.

If Hal and Winnie had felt their loneliness the last time Harold's plane flew out of sight, this time, their emotion was intensified by the fact that with the plane went a true and close friend, Bob Merchant.

Letters had been sent—letters Winnie had been busy writing while the men had gathered the roofing thatch, letters in answer to the ones she had received, and letters in anticipation of others she hoped to receive. Along with them went a note to Sally Merchant to express appreciation for the recipes and for lending her congenial husband to the lonesome missionary recruits for a couple of days.

When the plane left, they reluctantly turned their steps toward home on the rocky outcropping, Grandview. Winnie was watching the path ahead of them when she was brought up short by Hal's hand grasping her shoulder and pulling her to a halt. She heard him take a sharp breath and looked up to see what had startled him.

There, beside their bamboo house, at the edge of the compound stood four brown-skinned, nearly naked men.

10

Chapter

Morobukuni

KamApu watched the two strangers carefully. He saw the tall, pale-skinned man put his hand on the woman's shoulder as they both halted on the path. The wrinkled old man watched for any signs of hostility in the strangers, but he detected none. Rather, he noticed what appeared to be shocked surprise, then the couple resumed the walk toward their homestead, and toward their scantily clad visitors.

"Maba-ha'-hu," called the older man as the Fosters approached. The American couple did not know the meaning of the words, but guessed it to be a greeting, as later they would learn it to be. "Welcome," Hal replied, wondering if the excitement he felt was obvious to the Morobukuni men. Winnie sensed it. She could feel her husband's pulse beating strongly and rapidly as she gripped his arm with her hand.

The tallest of the men was the oldest one who had called the greeting. He was about as tall as Winnie. His hair was graying and wavy and cropped fairly close to his head. The wrinkles in his neck and face betrayed his age, but his arms, legs, and torso were lean and muscled, like that of a much younger man. The one thing that Hal and Winnie both noticed as they drew near were the tattoos encircling the man's arms and thighs. They looked like chains wrapped around and around.

The three younger men lacked the tattoos, but their dress was the same, a simple loincloth supported by a cord around the waist, but the buttocks of the men were openly displayed. They were also somewhat shorter than the older man. One of the men carried a short bow and had a quiver full of bamboo shafted arrows slung over his shoulder. The other two carried long reeds that Hal guessed were blowguns, for they were decorated with feathers and polished to a shine. The shortest but most muscular of the quartet carried a black wooden broad-bladed machete.

The older man thumped his chest and said, "KamApu."

Hal realized that the man was introducing himself, and Hal replied, with a thump on his own chest, "Hal." Then placing his hand on Winnie, Hal introduced her to KamApu. "Winnie," Hal said.

Each recognized in the other no malice or intent of harm, and soon all of them, the two Christian missionaries and the four loin-clothed Morobukuni, were chattering as if they expected their new acquaintances to understand every word. Little was gained from the conversation except the reassurance felt by all that this was not a dangerous confrontation. Hal continued to try to communicate with his new friends while Winnie went to the house to get her camera and tape recorder.

By the time Winnie returned, the Morobukuni men were no longer standing but had squatted, their buttocks resting on the backs of their ankles, and their knees thrust up against their chests. Hal had done his best to imitate their squat, but Winnie could tell he was not comfortable in that position. She sat in a more ladylike posture on a section of a log drawn up near the outdoor firepit.

She had brought some banana bread with her from the house and now offered it to her guests. The younger men watched the wrinkled oldster as he sniffed at the bread, then they grinned widely as he popped a large piece in his mouth, apparently with great pleasure. Very quickly the banana bread was but a happy memory, but the gift of food had intensified the friendliness of the natives.

As Hal tried to communicate with the men, Winnie took some pictures of the group, the Morobukuni and the American as well, gesturing and making hand motions as they spoke, each in his own language. Hoping to hear some words they could later translate, Winnie had pushed the *record* button on the cassette tape recorder she had in her bag, the same bag out of which she had produced the camera.

At one point in the conversation, old KamApu gestured toward the high mountain to the south of their peaceful valley, jabbering in his native tongue, somehow thinking that this outsider could surely understand at least part of what he said. "Your village?" Hal questioned. "Many houses?" he said as he pointed toward his own thatched-roof dwelling.

KamApu pointed toward the Fosters' house, then toward the mountain and made signs that indicated more than a dozen such houses might lie in the direction of the mountain. Hal was certain the old man was telling him that the Morobukuni village was beyond the mountain to the south.

Sensing that the visitors were getting ready to leave, Hal made motions to cause them to understand that they should wait for him. Then he rushed into the house and returned with a small hand-carved wooden cross which he gave to KamApu.

The old man responded with a grin, then reached into a pouch that was attached to the cord supporting his loincloth and produced a blowgun dart. He handed the dart to Hal, and the exchange of gifts was complete. The younger men nodded and grunted their approval.

Preparing to leave, the older man turned his gaze to the jungle cover near where the stream came out into the open meadow, but before he could turn completely away, Hal thrust out his hand to shake the hand of the dark-skinned, slightly built man. It was an unconscious move on Hal's part, spawned from years of American culture with no thought given to the fact that these Morobukuni men would know nothing of the customary European-American custom.

Surprised, the older man seemed first startled, then pleased, as he turned once more to face the tall young missionary. Hal was totally unprepared for what happened next. The man reached as if to clasp Hal's hand, but his reach went right on past the hand and he tightly gripped Hal's forearm. Hal's reaction was to grip the smaller man's forearm in the same way, and then to give a little startled jump as old KamApu leaped straight up into the air and uttered a shout, "Maba-ha'-hu!" The younger Morobukuni also leaped into the air. "Maba-ha'-hu!" they shouted. Then they laughed and pummeled each other on the back, and Hal was not spared this exuberant display of comradeship, being pummeled on the back as well. Unbeknownst to the young missionary, he had accidentally stumbled onto a custom of the tribe that went far to ensure his acceptance by them.

After the commotion of the strange "goodbye" subsided, the four brown men turned toward the forest. Hal and Winnie watched as they followed the trail alongside the stream until they were obscured from sight by the thick foliage.

"What an experience!" Winnie exclaimed. The visitors had been there less than an hour, but much had happened during that short time. It gave the young couple plenty to talk about for the rest of the day.

Hal reluctantly returned to the urgency of roof repair on the house. A taller ridge pole needed to be fastened to the existing ridge, which he accomplished by putting extensions on the bamboo center posts. Then more bamboo rafters would need to be fastened to the ridge pole, and appropriate stringers running parallel to the ridge down the slope of the roof. The roof improvements would take a few days to complete, but when it was finished, it did, indeed, prove to be well worth the extra effort. Never again did they have a problem with water dripping into the house from above.

As Hal resumed work on the roof, Winnie got out her sketch pad and recreated the scenes with their native visitors from memory. It wasn't hard to remember their clothing, for it consisted of only a cord around the waist with a long piece of rough-looking tan fabric looped over the cord at the front. She tried to remember each face and make the likenesses on the sketch pad as true as possible. She did well with it, for when taking a break from his work, Hal looked at her drawings and whistled a long, low approving whistle. He was very proud of his talented wife.

As the late afternoon sun dipped behind the top of the tall mountain ridge in the west, Hal and Winnie were preparing to eat their afternoon meal. Having departed from the schedule of civilization, they now ate only two meals each day, a large breakfast, and dinner late in the afternoon. They chattered excitedly about the visit of the Morobukuni as they ate, recalling as many details as they could about the day's events.

"Hal," Winnie said after a slight pause. "While I was sketching this afternoon, I remembered the story about Nate Saint and those four other missionaries who were killed by the Indians in Ecuador. Do you think we might be in danger from those men who were here today?" Her chin quivered and her voice shook as she finished the question.

"We will just have to trust the Lord to protect us," her husband said, in an effort to calm her fears. After noticing the weapons the Morobukuni carried, he too had been wondering about their safety. He had been nagged all afternoon as he worked on the roof with thoughts of concern for Winnie. *Had he been foolish and irresponsible to bring this lady he loved into such an uncertain way of life?*

Hoping to disguise his own uneasiness, Hal said, "I don't think the Lord would have brought us here just to have us killed. Those men were friendly, and I don't think they were afraid of us after they had been around us for a while. I believe we'll be all right." Hal hoped his words were a comfort and reassurance to Winnie. Nevertheless, for days afterward, they both cast troubled glances around them as they went about their daily activities.

One evening when the work on the thatched roof was nearly completed, they were having their usual prayer and Bible study time. Winnie let out a gasp as Hal was reading aloud their Scripture passage. "Hal," she interrupted, "That's it! We don't have to worry about the Morobukuni coming back to harm us!" Then she repeated the verse he had just read: "Do not fear, for I am with you; do not anxiously look about you, for I am your God. I will strengthen you, surely I will help you, surely I will uphold you with My righteous right hand" (Isaiah 41:10).

They slept peacefully that night and never worried again about harm coming from the people they had come to share God's truth with.

11
Chapter

Disappointment

A week had gone by since the visit of KamApu and his friends. Hal had finished remodeling the roof that afternoon. Normally, he would not have worked long in the afternoon heat, but by midday he was so nearly finished with the project that he couldn't stand to wait until the next day to finish it. Alternating between wiping perspiration from his eyes and tying palm fronds onto the roof near the peak, he finished late in the afternoon.

Exhausted, he climbed down the framework of the eastern gable and slid into the shade of the sleeping loft. Disdaining the softness of the bed he lay on the bamboo planked floor. He quickly drifted off to sleep but dozed fitfully until he heard Winnie's voice call from a great distance. Actually, she was bending over him, but in his restless yet fatigue drugged slumber, the sound of Winnie's greeting only seemed to be from afar.

"Wake up, Hal! Here, drink this. You should never have worked so hard in that heat! Do you want to leave me a lonely widow on this island?" she scolded. The tumbler of water felt cool and good in his hand, and he allowed some it to slop over the brim and spill on his chest as he drank. Winnie was right. He had pushed too hard to complete the roof. It could have waited another day. He lay back down, refreshed by the cool water, and finished his nap peacefully.

"Hal, we need an outhouse like the ones our grandparents had. The visitors we have had have all been men, and sometimes I need to tend to my own personal needs. We have been taking a spade with us to take care of our personal needs, and we usually go into bushes to do that, but I think we really need an outhouse."

Hal responded, "I hadn't thought about that. But I think you are right. You need privacy when you do your business, and you shouldn't have to take a spade with you into the bushes. It won't take me long to dig a pit for the outhouse and get that outhouse built. I think we really do need that outhouse." On the next day, Hal got that outhouse built.

"I think I'd like to plant a garden. Will you help me dig a garden plot?"

"A garden?" Hal answered. "I guess so. I hadn't thought about us being at this location long enough to harvest a garden."

"We built this house, didn't we? We must be planning to stay here for a while at least."

"Okay. I guess you're right. What will we plant?"

Winnie was ready with an answer. She had been thinking about this for some days now. "I have some squash and melon seeds packed away in our supplies, and some carrot and tomato seeds too. I get hungry for lettuce and cabbage. The next time Harold comes, I'm going to ask him to bring me some lettuce seeds and cabbage plants on his next trip."

"Well, I see you've got this thing all planned out. Have you picked a location for your garden yet?" Hal asked.

"Yes. I thought a good place would be a location below the spring along the little creek. During the dry season we could dig a small irrigation ditch to water it."

"Say, you really do have this figured out, don't you?" Hal said admiringly.

"Another thing," Winnie continued, "I would like to gather some of the native food plants and transplant them into our garden so we won't have to forage so much for the jungle foods. In time, I think we can have everything we need right here nearby. It would be good to plant a banana grove near the house, and I was also thinking it would be nice to have a few mango and papaya trees close by."

"Whoa, Nellie!" Hal laughed. "It sounds like a lot of work to me. But those are good ideas. I think we can probably get all these things done in time." The very next morning he spaded her garden plot for her.

For the next several days, the Fosters put themselves on a regular schedule. After an early breakfast, they would go out into the plain and into the edge of the jungle gathering edible plants to transplant into Winnie's garden. The very first morning after the garden had been spaded, Winnie planted a few short rows with the garden seeds she had brought from America. The balance of her garden would consist of the native transplants.

In the afternoons, when the heat became too intense to do much active work, they would replay the tape recording of the Morobukuni conversation they had recorded on the day of the native visit. They wrote down the syllables as they heard them, then using Hal's memories of what he guessed they were saying as he conversed with them, they put some possible meanings with the word groups they transcribed. Of one thing they were moderately certain, "Maba-ha'-hu" was a greeting, "hello" or something equivalent. "Poompa" was "mountain," Hal thought, and "tekkatu" was "house."

Day after day, they would listen to the tape, getting used to the syllabic flow of the Morobuku language. They wanted to be as ready as possible to learn the language when the opportunity came for them to spend more time with this tribe.

They saved the transplanting of the larger plants until last. One morning, Hal cut the tops off some small banana trees, then dug the roots up and transplanted them in scattered clumps near the house. The next morning, he located half a dozen small papaya trees and did the same with them, trimming the leaves off and planting just the trunks with their roots. In time, the trunks would sprout new leaves when the roots got over the shock of being transplanted. The banana groves would also later prove to be a great nearby food source. By the time the supply plane arrived again on the bay, the garden was completed and the trees transplanted.

True to his promise, Harold Gray had brought a notebook full of his wife's and her neighbor's recipes for Winnie. Now she would be able to add variety to what was becoming more and more a diet of native tropical foods.

The pilot approved of the improvements Hal had made on the roof of the house. He checked the thatch along the eaves and every place he could reach, then climbed to the sleeping loft and out the end and clambered his way to the peak of the roof where he once again checked the thatch.

"Good job, Hal," he said when he was once more on the ground, "You're a good worker, you are!"

Of course, the first thing the pilot encountered when he taxied his plane to the beach was two very excited young missionaries nearly stumbling over themselves in their eagerness to tell him about the visit of the Morobukuni. They told him every detail of the encounter, and when they had told everything, they began repeating themselves.

Hal gave Harold a sealed envelope addressed to the COP office in Port Moresby to be mailed when he returned to Bougainville. The envelope contained a full report of their first encounter with the island's native population. However, it had been four weeks since they had seen the native men. Were they never going to come back?

12
Chapter

Expedition

After Harold left with the floatplane, Hal and Winnie were concerned about the Morobukuni people. Should they try to find the village that KamApu seemed to say was over against the distant mountain? And what would they do if they found that village? Would the people of the village accept them as friends, or be nervous that these strangers might be dangerous enemies? The Morobukuni men seemed to be aware that Hal and Winnie were not hostile to them but actually were rather friendly to them. But what if the men who had visited the Foster home were not at the village when these missionaries came upon their village? How would the tribespeople receive them?

As the missionary couple thought about these things, they knew that nearly all of the primitive tribes worshipped and were afraid of evil spirits. Some tribes made sacrifices to the evil spirits, even human sacrifices. Some of the primitives honored the evil spirits as if they were gods. And there were evil spirits, demons, who took advantage of these primitive tribal groups.

Should the Fosters try to find that village, or should they wait until the Morobukuni sought them out again? To Hal, it seemed that they should try to find that village. They should make the long journey to try to find the village, take camping gear along if it took too long to find those people. Winnie agreed that they should go. They were both physically able to make the long trek, and Hal would have the heavier backpack, and Winnie would carry a smaller and lighter pack.

Their guess at the distant mountain could be at least ten miles from their home, and perhaps much farther than ten miles. That is why they decided to take their camping gear with them. As far as they knew, there were no dangerous animals on the Morobuku Island. There were probably wild pigs but no lions or leopards like there were in Africa. Perhaps the greatest danger they might face would be the very large monitor lizards that were in that region of New Guinea, but no one had indicated that any of the monitor lizards had ever been seen in Morobuku, especially those Komodo dragons.

As Hal and Winnie began their trek, they saw many colorful birds they could not identify. Hal took photos of so many different kinds of birds, and when Winnie had time, she also sketched some of these birds on her sketch pad. It was a beautiful place to be, but with no path to follow, some of the terrain they had to navigate was difficult, going through some jungle spaces and going through the tall grassy meadows. Their journey took longer than they had imagined.

Finally, they had to stop and make a camp. Had they actually traveled ten miles on their trek? It was hard to know how far they had gone on their first day. They had brought a small tent with them, but also brought two hammocks to sleep in. Hal built a fire, and Winnie put together a meal for them to eat before they turned in for the night. Sleeping became difficult for both of them, not knowing exactly where they were or if there were any dangers to be anticipated. Eventually, both of them fell asleep, and then awoke when the light of the morning began to brighten the sky.

Toward midday, they came to the base of the mountain KamApu had pointed toward, but there was no sign of a village. Going a little higher on the grade, they still saw no sign of any human habitation. There were no trails, no man-made clearings, just nothing that indicated any human interference with nature. What should they do? The only thing they could do was to return to their own home, which they could only reach by tomorrow.

On their homeward journey, they stumbled finally upon a human habitation, but it was a very old place. Apparently, it had been a Japanese camp when the soldiers were fighting against the allied forces in that region during World War II. When the Japanese were defeated by the allied forces, they abandoned that area, but there were still some walls that had collapsed from the dwellings that Japanese soldiers had built nearly forty years ago. That must have been what KamApu was trying to tell the Fosters, that there had been modern people who came to their island and had stayed there for a few years. This was not the site of their village, but rather the place where other civilized people had once made a camp.

Late in the day, the Fosters stopped again and made camp to spend the night. They slept better that night than the night before. Late the next day, they made their way home.

What were they to learn from the three-day jaunt into the unknown? They just had to be patient. If God wanted them to be on this island, to meet and evangelize this native people, God would lead them to the people He wanted them to meet. He would give them understanding of these people, and enable them to make friendship, and be able to share the good news to these tribal folks. Isn't that what they had come for? Was not the burning in their hearts that had led them to become missionaries to people who had never heard about Jesus's love for all the people in the world?

It would not be long before the Lord would give them that opportunity.

13

Chapter

Contact

Somewhat discouraged at being unable to locate a Morobuku village, the Fosters resumed their work on the limited vocabulary they had gleaned from their one-time encounter with those natives. They continued to try to determine what each word and each phrase the native men had said, but the Fosters had no idea what most of those terms meant. Hopefully, they could eventually learn to communicate with these people.

When the monthly flight came with Harold's supplies, Harold had some good news for Hal and Winnie. Harold, on his last trip to the Fosters, having left them, had flown along the coastline of the island. He had seen smoke, which he assumed had come from cooking fires. As he neared the smoke, he flew up a river about three miles and saw a village. The village was a cluster of three longhouses, and it was only about ten miles and two ridges distant from the Fosters' home.

"Wow!" Hal exclaimed. "We could make that trek in only one day. We could camp at the mouth of the river and would only be three miles from the village. When you come next month, Harold, meet us at the mouth of that river." Hal was excited. Winnie was excited, and their excitement spilled over into Harold as well. And

Harold, sharing that good news with the Fosters, stayed a few hours before he flew back to Bougainville. He had come to love that young missionary couple.

After Harold left, the Fosters held hands and bowed in prayer. What deep feelings they both felt. Their souls were comforted by the presence of the Lord who had brought them to this place. For many minutes, they continued in prayer. They rejoiced in the opportunity the Lord had given them.

When they came out of that time of prayer, Hal had something to say. "I think we should go to the mouth of that river only about a week before Harold comes back with our monthly supplies. Three weeks from now, we will plan to go to that place and make a camp near the mouth of that river. We don't know if that village is the only village of the Morobukuni, but I assume there may be other villages also. We will just have to wait and find out if there are any other villages. In the meantime, we will do our best to prepare for the meeting with that one village Harold told us about."

Winnie accepted Hal's advice about waiting for three weeks prior to going to that location. They would need to do a lot of prayer time and use the time to go through the words they had on their tape recorder that the natives had uttered. Surely, the Lord would give them some understanding of those words, and hopefully, when they actually met those villagers, they would get more understanding from them. Time would tell.

After three weeks of preparation, the time had come for the Fosters to begin their journey to that mouth of the river near where the villagers lived. Starting out, they crossed the riffle on the creek and continued on their journey. Again, Hal carried the heavier pack. They were going through the jungle, but following a ridge made it easier for them to get to their destination. The jungle wasn't as dense on the top of the ridge.

It took one long day for them to get to the mouth of the river where it emptied into a small bay. When they arrived, they set up their camp, ate a quick snack, and were very tired. They were hoping to rise in the morning with the intention of finding the village upstream. When they woke the next morning, they saw a Morobuku man and two women squatting by their campfire. They were ready to lead the Fosters to their village.

The three Morobukuni led the Fosters to their village, but the village was about three miles from Hal and Winnie's camp at the mouth of the river, so it took about an hour to get there. The village consisted of three great longhouses designed to house about fifty people in each. The longhouses were built on stilts, with a floor a few feet off the ground, and pigs and jungle foul could be on the ground while the families could be off the ground. The roofs were palm thatch just like the Foster house. And in the longhouses, there were spaces for the families of men, women, and children, and many of these men had more than one wife, so the family groups in the longhouse could be somewhat large.

Then Hal and Winnie recognized KamApu. He had Hal's wooden cross around his neck, suspended by a cord. Obviously, KamApu and his three companions had told the village about seeing these white-skinned people on the other side of the island, and apparently, these white-skinned people were friendly. When the Fosters arrived at the mouth of the river, it did not take long for the Morobuku people to know that they were nearby.

The men were dressed just like the four men who had visited the Fosters' house, with a cord around the waist and a flap of some kind of material covering their genitals. The women wore grass skirts about to mid-thigh but were bare from the waist up. Most of the children, especially the smaller children, were completely naked, male and female.

There were clay stew pots over fires between the three longhouses, and anyone who was hungry could reach into the stew pots and retrieve something to eat, whether vegetable or something of an animal. That is the way these natives lived. They shared everything.

The Fosters were given a tour of each of the longhouses, and Winnie had brought her tape recorder along in the bag she carried, hoping to glean more words from these people so that, eventually, Hal and Winnie could learn their language. Hammocks were stretched one over another in family groups, and these family groups had a little separation from other family groups but not that much space between them. It was not a very clean place. It had many odors that were not pleasant. The Morobukuni knew nothing of germs or microbes. Winnie, with some of her nurse training, noticed some of the people lying in hammocks that did not seem to be very well. After being led through the first house, Hal and Winnie were not that excited about seeing the other longhouses, but their guides led them through each one.

Having been given the grand tour of the village, Hal and Winnie wondered why they were shown each of the longhouses. Perhaps they would understand that someday, but not today. It was very puzzling to the Fosters that the Morobukuni were not more private about their personal affairs. It was surprising that the tribal elders had allowed them to see their living style, even guiding them through the long-houses. Was there an ulterior motive in that decision?

Of course, the women and children were kept at a distance during that tour of the village. It was the men who led the Fosters, particularly the older men. The older and more experienced men ruled the village, but perhaps the reason they were allowed to go through their homes was that KamApu had begun to trust the missionaries. Of course, these Morobukuni people had no idea that the Fosters were Christian missionaries. They had never heard of Christianity. The cross Hal had given to KamApu was simply a talisman to that man.

As the men tried to communicate with Hal, Winnie left and went toward the women and children, and these women were very curious about this white woman, especially since she was completely clothed. Were white women built the same way as Morobukuni women were? Could they touch her skin to see if it felt like their own skin? Winnie allowed them to touch her. She wanted to get to know these women even though she had no knowledge of what they were saying. But these native women were excited to see a white woman they had never seen before. Some of the government officials they had seen from a distance, but those officials never had any women with them.

Hal tried to communicate with the men by pointing at an object and saying his English word for the object, and the men caught on quickly, saying in their own language the name of that object. This was a blessing, for the men then began pointing to objects and saying the name of the objects. Winnie was doing the same with the women, and she had her tape recorder with her, having reached down into her bag and turning on the recorder so she and Hal could later replay those words.

Later in the day, Hal indicated to the men that he and Winnie would like to return to their own camp, and the men were agreeable with that. They, however, were very curious about the reason these white people had come to their village.

As Hal and Winnie made their way back to their camp by the mouth of the river, some of the men walked with them for part of the way, but then went back to their own village. When the Fosters were alone, they began talking about all the things they had seen and experienced in the village. These people were not all that different from the Mika people except that they were a little lighter-skinned than the Mikas. Major Billup had told them that the Morobukuni were more like the Maori people of New Zealand. But they were still primitive people, and they lived off the land, harvesting what the land provided with fruits and yams and birds and pigs and lizards.

When the Fosters got back to their camp, Hal suggested that when Harold came to their campsite, Hal and Winnie would ask Harold to take them back to their own home. By the time Harold would get there, the Fosters would have been near the village for nearly a week.

It was time now for Hal and Winnie to get to their food. They had not eaten since last evening and were hungry. They left their camp in the morning because the Morobukuni people were ready to lead them, and Hal and Winnie got no breakfast. Of course, they did not eat out of the cooking pots at the village. They had no idea what was in those pots, and that food would not have been sanitary.

On the next day, the Fosters returned to the village. They were praying that there would be some way they could learn more of the language of these people, and they also wanted to be friendly; and if they saw any need they observed, they could reach out to meet those needs. The Lord would have to provide the opportunity. Hal went to the men, and Winnie went to the women and children.

On the fourth day of their visit to the Morobuku village, something happened that Hal and Winnie were not prepared for. There were loud and angry voices coming from the second longhouse. A man was shouting at a woman and a young child, and that woman and child were being evicted from their hammocks. The Fosters did not know how to react to that situation. The child may have been ten or eleven years of age, and apparently, the child had done something that his father could not tolerate. Both mother and child were driven from the longhouse, and the other Morobukuni would have nothing to do with them. They were being shunned by the entire tribal group. They had no place to go.

Hal looked at Winnie. "Should we interfere with this situation?" Hal asked. "We came to help these people, so should we just ignore this problem? Would helping this mother and child be the wrong thing to do?"

Winnie replied, "Let's go away a little distance from the village and pray about this." They did, and it seemed after their prayer time that they should involve themselves with the woman and child.

As they went to the woman and child, they made motions that they were willing to help them. Both the woman and child were terrified about how they had been treated by their fellow villagers, and when the Fosters reached out to them, the mother and child were willing to go with them to their campsite.

As they were leaving the village, going down the river shore, a man they had never seen before pursued them. The woman and child knew who the man was and were extremely terrified. The man was not her husband. He had many tattoos on his body and had decorations and amulets and bones hanging around his neck on cords that the Fosters had never seen before. Hal guessed that this man may be the village witch doctor, a shaman, and shamans could cast evil spells on people through the power of demons. The shaman came up to Hal and shouted at him, and made signs, and held amulets toward Hal. But nothing happened to Hal. The shaman thought Hal would faint or swoon or fall down because of his magic, but Hal was not fazed. Hal was protected by the Holy Spirit.

Then the shaman turned toward Winnie. The shaman knew women were much weaker than men, and the shaman did the same thing he had done to Hal, but Winnie was not troubled in any way. The shaman was defeated, and some of the villagers who were watching that performance were amazed that nothing bad had happened to the Fosters. Even the woman and child could not believe what had just happened. Everyone in the village knew they could be put under the witch doctor's spells...except Hal and Winnie. The shaman went away defeated and ashamed.

When the Fosters took with them the woman and child and went to their camp, they gave the two natives a place to sleep for the night and gave them some of their food. Could this be a way that Hal and Winnie could learn the dialect of the Morobukuni people?

On the following day, Harold arrived, and there was room in his plane for the four people and Hal and Winnie's camping gear. The native woman and her child were very fearful when they got into Harold's plane, and even more fearful when the plane left the water into the air. At first, the child was terrified, but when they were airborne the child became really excited as he looked out the window and saw the sea and the land beneath them. What an experience for two Stone Age people to see the land and sea in a way they had never seen them before.

Winnie had learned that the native woman's name was Pupa, and her child's name was Boka.

KamApu had gone to see what the Fosters and Pupa and Boka would do, and then he saw the plane land in the mouth of the river. He had never seen such a sight before; it looked like a huge bird because it could fly. As he watched, he noticed that Hal and Winnie and Pupa and Boka went to that huge bird, and then the bird seemed to swallow them. Do these huge birds swallow people? Or are these people, these white-skinned people...are they gods? This was very unsettling to KamApu. Who were they, and what kind of people had he befriended?

14
Chapter

Getting Acquainted

When Harold went around the Morobuku Island to Hal and Winnie's home, these native people were mesmerized by the experience they had endured, the woman and the boy. Winnie tried to comfort them through the short twenty-minute flight to their own bay. Pupa was very frightened by the experience, but Boka had become ecstatic with this first-time-ever experience. What kind of people were these who had taken his mother and him into their custody? They were very different from any people he had ever seen before, and the man holding on to that round thing in the huge bird…what kind of person was he?

When Harold floated the plane up to the beach, he helped his passengers out and offered to help them carry their supplies to their house. To Boka, he looked different from the people who had rescued him and his mother from their own people. He was similar to them, but different.

Harold was somewhat troubled by what the Fosters had done. Were they going to have problems with the tribe they had just visited because they took a woman and a boy with them to their own home? Harold knew that sometimes these Stone Age natives had peculiar ideas about their own people. He wanted to help the Fosters as much as he could, but would they even be alive when he returned in another month?

When the boy and mother saw the house Hal and Winnie had built, it was not at all like the longhouse they had lived in all of their lives. It was different. It was not taller than their longhouse; but it was more square than long. It had no hammocks hanging from the rafters, but it did have a bamboo floor like their longhouse had.

Hal got out their hammocks and strung them under the floor of their own sleeping chamber so Pupa and Boka would have a place to sleep. Winnie began gathering yams to make a meal for the four of them plus Harold, but Harold wanted to talk to Hal and Winnie about the decision they had made to bring the woman and child to their own house. Hal and Winnie explained that the village had exiled Pupa and Boka, and the Fosters wanted to help them. They only thing they could think of was to bring them with them to Grandview. A plus about this situation was that Pupa and Boka might help the Fosters to learn the Morobukuni language.

When Harold went to his floatplane, he felt a little better about the decision Hal and Winnie had made, but he was still uneasy about what might happen. He would have to let the constabulary know about this situation, but Hal had already given him a letter to the powers that be, explaining their decision. Another letter Hal had given was a plea to the missionaries in Papua New Guinea about sending someone to help them with the language situation, at least for a few weeks or a month. These people had been translating the languages of their own people and were far more experienced than Hal and Winnie were. Hal and Winnie had taken classes in their linguistics study on translating a new language, but it would help tremendously if one or more of their friends could spend some time with them.

As the day went by, Pupa and Boka began to relax and began to realize that these white people had not kidnapped them but were kind to them because of the problem they had in their own village. However, Hal and Winnie still did not know what the boy had done to cause his mother and him to be banished from the tribe, or maybe it was something the mother had done. Hopefully, as they began to learn the tribal language, they would eventually find out what that problem was that caused Pupa and Boka to be cast out of their village.

As the next few days passed, Winnie worked with Pupa, and Hal worked with Boka as they did their particular chores around the Foster home. But as they did these chores, they would point at an object and learn what the Morobukuni word was for that object, whether it was a fruit or vegetable, or some other object. Both Hal and Winnie kept a pad with them to record the words these natives used to identify whatever the Fosters were pointing at. And the natives wondered what those markings were. Finally, they realized that the Fosters were trying to learn their language.

The estimated time to learn the language of a native and illiterate culture was at least a few years for the missionaries to be able to speak fluently in that primitive language. Hal and Winnie knew that already, and they were dedicated to that task so that, eventually, they would be able to tell these people that God loved them and that Jesus had given His own life for them. It would take patience and fortitude to see this task out to fruition.

More days went by with Hal working on the house where work was needed, and both Hal and Winnie would work in their garden along with Pupa and Boka. The more time the natives worked alongside the Fosters, they became more relaxed and less fearful, and they wanted Hal and Winnie to learn their language. They used every opportunity to share their words, pointing to something and saying its name. They told the Fosters their names for the plants in the garden, and when a bird appeared, they spoke their name for the bird. Also, they occasionally saw large and small rats, and they had special names for them.

As Hal and Winnie gathered more words from the natives living with them, they would try to use the words they had learned, but both Pupa and Boka laughed when they mispronounced the word they were trying to say. The natives would then repeat the proper pronunciation of the word, and because of the way these natives said the word, with its proper inflection, it was difficult for the Fosters to get it said in the correct way. However, they had fun with their mispronunciations. They were learning some of the language, but they had so much more to learn.

Both Hal and Winnie had been in the longhouses of the Morobuku tribe and knew that those longhouses had a bamboo floor a few feet off the ground. Where Hal had hung the hammocks for Pupa and Boka, the ceiling of that room was eight feet off the ground, and Hal decided to put a bamboo floor about a foot off the ground so the Morobukuni would feel more comfortable in their sleeping chamber. In two days, Hal was able to get that done for these Morobukuni who were now living with them.

As time went by, Pupa had always wondered why the white woman was not naked from the waist up. Pupa wore a grass skirt but had no clothing above that grass skirt. One time, Pupa reached out and touched Winnie's fabric, and Winnie realized that Pupa was curious about her clothing. With sign language, which was the only way Winnie could really communicate with Pupa, Winnie tried to ask Pupa if she would like to have clothing like Winnie wore. Soon Pupa understood what Winnie was trying to ask her: Would Pupa like to wear something like Winnie wore? Yes! Yes! Pupa would like to see how that would be for her.

Now Pupa was smaller and shorter than Winnie. Could Winnie make something that Pupa could wear comfortably? Winnie decided to make a shift dress for the native woman out of material Winnie had in her supplies. That might work, and Winnie, in a short time made that little dress for Pupa. When Pupa dropped her skirt and slid into that dress, Pupa became excited. She laughed. She was happy. She was covered from her shoulders all the way down to her knees. She had never dressed that way before. None of the Morobukuni women were ever dressed like she was now.

After Hal saw Pupa in that dress that Winnie had made, he wondered if he should put Boka into some shorts, although Hal's shorts were much too big for the eleven-year-old boy. Could Winnie take one of Hal's khaki shorts and make two pairs of shorts for the young stripling? Sure, she could; Winnie was pretty handy with needle and thread.

When Boka saw his mother in that new dress, he was really surprised. He wondered if he could be clothed like his mother was. It was not long before Winnie had taken a pair of Hal's shorts and had made one pair of shorts for Boka out of one leg of Hal's shorts. That kid was really small, and she could make another pair of shorts for Boka out of the other leg of Hal's shorts.

Soon both Pupa and Boka looked more modern than they had looked in their old way of dressing. Both Hal and Winnie noticed that when they were with the Mika tribe at Bob and Sally's ministry in Papua New Guinea, some of the Mika people had adopted the modern clothing that their missionaries wore. Some of the men wore shorts, and some of the women wore simple shift dresses like Winnie had made for Pupa.

15
Chapter

Natives Troubled

KamApu spoke to two other leaders of their village, Koopa and Badi. KamApu and Koopa and Badi were very concerned about what had happened. They had seen how their shaman was troubled when he tried to cast spells on Hal and Winnie. The Fosters were not fazed by the shaman's effort to cast a demonic curse on them. The shaman had never had anyone react the way the Fosters had. They were not troubled at all when the shaman had done his best to curse them with demonic spirits. The shaman's magic, done through demonic forces, had always put his own people in danger. Some died immediately after he cast his spell, and others would become dangerously ill, but not those white strangers.

Koopa and Badi had not seen the Fosters and two of their own people go into the floatplane, but KamApu had seen it and had already told the men in their village about that. The Morobukuni people had seen planes, which the Morobukuni thought were birds, fly over their island at a great high distance, but this floatplane, piloted by Harold Gray, they had never seen before. It looked like a huge bird, but it was different from a bird. Its wings did not flap, and it made a horrible noise, a noise so loud that it hurt the natives' ears.

Then KamApu told the Morobukuni men that Hal and Winnie and Pupa and Boka went to that monster bird, that the bird seemed to swallow those four people. And then that monster bird left with a very loud noise. What were these native people supposed to think about that experience? After KamApu told the men about what he had witnessed, some of the younger men raced down to the mouth of the river, and the white people's camp was no longer there. Pupa and Boka were no longer there. Fear clutched at these men's stomachs.

KamApu, Koopa, and Badi, who were the main leaders of the village, made a decision: Two of the younger men who had visited the Fosters' home several weeks ago would take a couple of other men with them to see if the white people were back at their home. If that monster bird had swallowed them, these white people and Pupa and Boka would never be seen again. But if the white people, and even Pupa and Boka were at that house, then there must be some kind of reason why they survived that terrible bird.

The Morobukuni natives had seen other white people, but they always came in a very large canoe. Their canoes were much larger than the canoes the Morobukuni people had made for themselves. They were broader, but not that much longer than the dugout canoes the natives used to go up rivers or even out into the open water. But never had the natives seen a bird as large as the one that showed up on that day when Hal and Winnie left their village.

It took at least a half day for the four men to go see if the white people were at their home. Standing far enough away in the foliage of the jungle, the four men witnessed that the white people were back at their home, and also, Pupa and Boka were there. Not wanting the people they were looking at to discover them, these four men left and went back to their village, and by nightfall, they were already at their village.

"What should we do about these white people?" KamApu said to the men of the village. "Should we go and try to rescue Pupa and Boka from them, or should we leave them alone?" Some of the men knew what Boka had done to anger the gods. Boka had violated a very sacred place. When his father discovered Boka's evil deed, he cast Boka and Pupa from his lodgings in the longhouse. Pupa had tried to rescue Boka from his father's anger, so both Pupa and Boka were banished from their people.

"No, no! Pupa and Boka should never be allowed back into any of our longhouses because of what Boka had done," shouted more than one of the men who were gathered in that official meeting. Of course, women and children were not allowed to attend a meeting like this. This was the men's business. The men ruled in this village.

"Then what should we do?" Koopa said.

Badi, one of the village elders, said, "We must ask the spirits what to do about this. The spirits will tell us what to do." Most of the men nodded in agreement, and even KamApu agreed with that.

As far as the Morobukuni knew, they were *The People*. They had been on this land for many generations, and the land had been very good to them. No one, even the oldest of *The People,* could ever remember how *The People* came to this land. They had always been here in this land. This was their home. This was their land. They had fish to eat, yams and other foods in the jungle, and they were able to raise pigs and hunt for the birds and rats and even the monitor lizards. They were good food for *The People.*

Why had these white people come to *The People's* land? What was their motive? They had already tried to learn some of the words *The People* spoke, but *The People* could understand nothing of what these white people spoke. Their words made no sense to these natives, these aboriginal Stone Age people. Why were these white people here on our land? They did not seem to be dangerous people. They seemed to be friendly. But why had they come?

KamApu said, "I think we should leave these people alone. They live a day's march from our village, and the other two villages are farther from them than we are. We have never had enemies, and I do not believe that these white-skinned people are our enemies. We do not know why they are here in our land, but let us leave them alone. Let us see if they will ever try to come back to our village."

Most of the men agreed with KamApu. A few of the men were doubtful, but all agreed to leave the white people alone. "Let them live in their part of the land, and we will live in our part of the land," Badi said.

16
Chapter

A New Helper

The Fosters received a letter from Ed Hart that told them that they would be getting another helper, Sarah Graves, from the United States. Hal and Winnie had sent a letter a few months before that they would like to have another helper to help learn the language of the Morobukuni people. When Winnie learned that another woman would come to help with the language learning, Winnie was excited. It would be wonderful to have another woman to talk to. Even though she had Pupa, she could not really have that much communication with her. They had not really learned each other's languages yet.

Now that Harold Gray was coming only every other month, Hal would have no man friend to visit with, but when Harold came, Hal had another guy to visit with. Winnie was deprived of a visit with another woman, especially an American woman.

Sarah was a new addition to the mission team, but she had been in South America with another mission team, learning a language from the Tunebo people. When some New Testament books were translated for the tribe she was working with, it was time for her to seek another group to work with. She knew there was much work to do in Papua New Guinea, and she sought a group she could work with there.

Bob and Sally Merchant and Sid and Molly Craft already had some extra help on their translation team, so with the Merchants and Crafts and Harts' agreement, Sarah was to go to the Fosters to help them learn the language and eventually translate that language of the Morobukuni people. Hal and Winnie already had two Morobukuni living with them, so they could learn the language from these natives. But Sarah, who had much experience in learning languages in South America, would be a great help to the Fosters. They would be able to learn the language much quicker and be able to teach the Morobukuni people about how much God loved them.

It would be about a month before Sarah would join the Fosters. She would have to have clearance from the Council on Primitives office in Port Moresby.

Winnie was so excited to have another woman who spoke the English language to be with her, probably for several years, because it usually took several years to learn the language of primitive people and share the Word of God with them. "Hal," Winnie excitedly said, "we need to get a new room added to our house so Sarah Graves will have her own private room. Could you do that for me, oh, I mean for her?" Hal grinned at her comment and was willing to do anything for her, within reason.

Hal replied, "I think we have enough time to get an addition onto this house. We already have Pupa and Boka living beneath our own room, and I have been thinking that we may need to build another room. But how about giving Sarah our old room and build another room for ourselves? Would that be okay with you?"

On the very next day, Hal began working on the supplies he would need to build that other room. He took Boka with him, and they went to find the thicker bamboo poles that would give that extra room stability. They would also need smaller bamboo poles for a ceiling and for the floors, and medium-sized poles for the floor joists. Hal had done this kind of thing before, and he had gained experience through what he had to do now.

As Hal and Boka gathered their supplies, Boka would see a bird and give its name to Hal. There were so many colorful birds in their area—kingfishers, doves, and parrots, and many other kinds.

Although Hal was not as excitable as Winnie, he still liked to see these amazing birds of many different colors and loved to hear the sounds they made in the jungle…except that screamer bird. He hoped he would never hear that birdcall again.

Boka began seeing Hal as his own father. Boka knew his own father, but his own father had disowned him. Hal was a much nicer man than Boka's father was. Hal treated Boka like a loving father would treat his own son, sometimes correcting the child, but most of the time loving the son. Hal and Boka had developed a real relationship with each other, and Boka was happy to be with his *new father*.

The boy shared words with his *new father* so this *new father* could learn how to communicate with him, and one day, as they were working together, gathering the supplies they would need to build the addition to the house, Hal spoke of the Morobukuni people. The boy did not understand that word, and Hal tried to explain, through sign language and gestures, that he was talking about Boka's people. The boy shook his head. In his own language, he said, "No! Morobukuni not right. We are 'The People' (Tomaka)!" Boka pointed to himself and said, "Tomaka, Tomaka." And at first, Hal thought Boka was correcting his own name, but then Hal realized that Boka did not call himself a Morobukuni; he was saying the actual name of his own native people, Tomaka.

Of course, Hal did not fully realize what Boka was trying to tell him, but he knew the boy was trying to tell him something important. Hal tucked that word, Tomaka, into his memory so he could speak it to Winnie and to Pupa. But he and Boka had a lot of work to do that day, gathering the materials they would need to build on that addition to their house.

Prior to the time Sarah was to join the Fosters, Hal, with the young boy's help, got that extra room built onto their house. Boka was a great help to Hal. Boka would hold a bamboo pole in place while Hal would secure it. Prior to Pupa and Boka joining Hal and Winnie, Winnie had to do the work that the young boy was now doing. That was a great relief to Hal so that Winnie could do what a woman normally does.

Day by day, Hal and Winnie gleaned a few words from the natives living with them. By evening of that day, when they sat down to eat their dinner, Hal mentioned the word *Tomaka*. Pupa and Boka pointed to each other, and then to themselves. They were Tomaka. Then they said "Tomaka" and circled their arms to indicate that their tribe and their families were all Tomaka. Morobuku was the name of the island these people were living on, but their tribal name was Tomaka. But it would take more time for Hal and Winnie and Sarah, who was soon to join them, that Tomaka meant "*The People.*"

Back at the Tomaka village, things went along the way they nearly always went. The shaman, if he became angry or disapproved of some of the people, would cast a spell on them. The shaman's power came from demonic sources, and those demonic forces could cause people to become extremely ill. If someone called for the shaman to heal their illness, they would have to pay for his services with whatever they had to give. If the shaman agreed to their payment, he might be able to relieve them of their suffering, even if their suffering came from a demonic spell the shaman had cast on them.

However, some of the illnesses did not come from a spell the shaman had cast on someone. It could be malaria, or an infection from a wound caused by a simple accident or any other illness people in tropical climates could come down with. The shaman was well known for his power to heal illness, although many times his power did not heal any illness. Sometimes, his treatment made the illness become even worse than it had been before. He used bat and lizard dung, poultices from many different plants, and sometimes the shaman would bleed the patient. That bleeding sometimes caused an infection around the place of the bleeding, and then the patient could become even more sickly.

These Tomaka people had lived in this environment for many generations. They knew which plants were poisonous, and they knew which plants were useful. They had learned which animals were good to eat and which animals they should not try to eat. They knew the reptiles, they knew the birds, and they were well aware of the bats that frequented their area. Many of those bats were creatures that ate fruit, and you could usually find these creatures near the trees that bore the fruit these bats loved.

The Tomaka people also believed in legends and demons. They had many stories about the people in the spirit world. When Satan finds a people that do not know the God of love, the old devil puts evil things in these people's minds. The Tomaka people had traditions that were harmful to these people. Satan hates humans whom God had made in His own image, and the devil persecutes these people with many wicked devices. That is why demons seek a person of a particular tribe, who knows nothing of the God of love, so they can use that person to be a constant trouble to their people. Demons usually dwell in a shaman who has been trained to accept these demonic forces.

Such were the people whom the Fosters were trying to reach out to, to share with them the God of love; to share with them the Son of God who went to the cross of Calvary to redeem them. God had sent the Fosters because God loved these people.

17
Chapter

The Helper Arrives

When the Fosters heard the hum of the seaplane, they became excited to finally meet their new missionary. They had already built a new room onto their house to make it more comfortable for Sarah Graves.

As the Fosters went down to the beach to meet Harold Gray and their new missionary partner, they were pleasantly surprised to see Ed and Mary Hart getting out of the plane and onto the beach. Ed and Mary had decided to accompany Sarah to the place the Fosters were living. The Fosters had been living there for nearly a year. It would be good to see Hal and Winnie again and to be able to introduce Sarah Graves to them. Of course, Ed and Mary would take the flight back to Bougainville with Harold, but only after spending a few hours with Hal and Winnie and Sarah.

Sarah was in her midforties while Hal and Winnie were in their early thirties. What wisdom Sarah would bring with her, and having been a registered nurse for most of her career, that would be a special blessing to the Fosters. Winnie had studied to become a nurse but did not finish her studies to even become a licensed practical nurse. So with Sarah and her medical experience, this would be a great blessing to the Fosters and also to the Tomaka people they would hopefully become acquainted with in the future.

After the introductions had been made between the Fosters and Sarah, they all went along the path to Hal and Winnie's home. When Ed saw the house Hal had built, he was impressed with what Hal had accomplished. As they drew nearer to the house along the path, Mary also noticed how good that house looked, made of bamboo and palm thatch. Ed remarked, "Hal, you have done a great job building your home. With the local materials at hand, you have made this a comfortable house."

Hal replied, "Well, part of the reason it was built this way is because Harold gave me some valuable pointers. I had made some mistakes, and Harold helped me correct those mistakes."

As the men talked, the ladies were ready to get alone and away from the guys. Winnie was so excited to share conversations with her friend, Mary, and was extremely pleased in meeting Sarah. The gals went up into the rooms in the house, and the guys were examining all the work Hal and Boka had done to build the new addition.

Ed remarked, "Hal, have you been able to learn some of the language of the Morobukuni people?"

Hal replied, "Well, we thought they were Morobukuni, but we recently found that they don't call themselves Morobukuni. They refer to themselves as the Tomaka people. When I spoke to Boka, the little boy living with us, Boka replied in his own tongue, 'No Morobukuni! Tomaka! Tomaka!'"

Ed thought about that and said to Hal, "Many of the tribes refer to themselves as 'The People,' especially if they have no nearby neighbors. That may be the translation for Tomaka, but you can learn about that as you get more acquainted with their language." Actually, Tomaka was the name for "The People," and Hal and Winnie and Sarah would eventually realize that Tomaka meant "The People."

As Mary and Winnie visited with Sarah, these women quickly became very good friends, and it was necessary that Winnie should regard Sarah as a special friend, for they would be working together and living together for, hopefully, the next several years. These ladies hit it off really well together, and Sarah had been hoping that she would fit in well with the Fosters. Sarah had the experience of having been a missionary for over twenty years, and Hal and Winnie would need her experience.

"Winnie," Sarah exclaimed. "I am so glad you have adopted these natives into your own family. It must have been God who arranged that for you. This mother and son will help you learn their language." Sarah had heard about these people Hal and Winnie had adopted, but she had not yet seen them.

With these other white people coming to the Fosters' home, Pupa and Boka went to the jungle to get away from these strange people. It was more than this mother and son could bear, being around these strangers, so they hid themselves until these people went away. But were they all here to stay? Pupa and Boka had become used to Hal and Winnie, but they were nervous when these other white people arrived.

Winnie explained, "We felt we had no choice. This mother and son were being banished from their own people, and Hal and I went to pray about what we should do. It became very clear to us that we needed to rescue these people, and yes, I think God definitely had a hand in this matter."

Sarah was perhaps an inch taller than Winnie and perhaps a little bit slenderer than Winnie. She appeared to be healthy and had a sharp eye that noticed things in her environment. She also seemed to have an energy that others could see in her. Winnie thought Sarah would be a great help to her and Hal.

When Sarah was in a Christian college prior to going to the mission field, she had a steady boyfriend, and they seemed to become somewhat serious in their relationship. But when Gary, the boyfriend, learned that Sarah was seriously considering the mission field, and especially to people who had never heard the gospel of Christ, he began to become somewhat cool in their relationship. Gary did not want to become a missionary. He hoped to become a minister in a church in the United States.

After Sarah graduated, she went to the Summer Institute of Linguistics, in Arkansas, in order to become more proficient in language study. If she was going to try to reach Stone Age people, she would need to learn how to translate the language these people used. How else could she show the love of Christ to the people she would be going to?

Before Ed and Mary Hart left, the missionaries had a prayer session, and even Harold Gray joined in. Harold was already a believer in Christ, and he and his wife attended a church in Bougainville. He had a strong affection for the Fosters. The Harts knew how long it might take for the Fosters and Sarah Grace to learn the people's language; they had been through this before, and so had Sarah.

It had been a thrilling blessing to Hal and Winnie that the Harts accompanied Sarah to her new location with the Fosters. Sarah had been with the Harts until she had received her clearance from the Council on Primitives office, and that took a few weeks. These officials had to look at Sarah's time in South America, and they had to contact the people Sarah had worked with, but this all came out just fine. Sarah passed their scrutiny with flying colors.

After the floatplane left, Hal and Winnie gave Sarah a grand tour of their home, and Hal deposited Sarah's gear into her own room. Sarah had brought not only her own clothing but books and even recording equipment. Her recording equipment was a full-size reel-to-reel tape recorder that ran on batteries, and they were large batteries, which would enable Sarah to use her tape recorder for extended periods of time. However, they would have to get more batteries from time to time when Harold would deliver their monthly supplies.

Of course, Winnie had already shown Sarah the room she would be staying in. It had a cot made from bamboo where Sarah could sleep, and it reminded Sarah of the structure where she had stayed when she was in South America. But the room seemed comfortable. She thought she would enjoy the years that she planned to be with Hal and Winnie.

Finally, Pupa and Boka arrived, having seen the plane leave, and they were not surprised by the presence of Sarah. They realized that someone else was coming when Hal and Boka built that other room onto their house. But they were a little shy when they saw Sarah.

She was a new white person joining their family. Would she be there for a short time, or would she become a permanent member of the family? When Sarah reached out to them, they became comfortable with Sarah's presence. Winnie came to Pupa and Boka and told them Sarah's name and introduced Sarah to the mother and child. Sarah was pleased to meet these natives. She could learn their language in the coming months and years, and she knew she would come to love them.

Later in the day, Hal and Winnie and Pupa and Boka gave Sarah a tour of their garden that they had made across the creek. They showed her the native plants in the garden but also the North American plants—radishes, lettuce, and carrots that were growing in the garden. Sarah was surprised that the Fosters had banana trees and mango trees near the garden. They had done well in gathering the native plants, transplanting them where they could produce those fruits for them.

As they returned to the house to eat an evening meal, Sarah had already noticed the outhouse that Hal had built for the enlarged family. That would be a blessing to both Sarah and Winnie.

After the evening meal, which was eaten under the shade of the trees surrounding the site, Hal and Winnie showed the words they had gathered from Pupa and Boka, and they also shared some of the recordings Winnie had made with her small cassette recorder. This would be the basis for the project they would be working on for the next months and years.

As the days went by, Hal, Winnie, and Sarah had many conversations about how to reach out to the Tomaka people. Sarah shared many stories about the Tunebo people she had worked with in South America. Sometimes, their conversations went another way, talking about the places they had lived in America, how their college classes had gone, and how each of them had decided to become missionaries. These times together molded them into a family atmosphere.

Then as the weeks went by, Sarah and Winnie worked with Pupa to learn as much of the language as they could. They would point at an object and Pupa, knowing what they were trying to do, would say the Tomaka word for the object. Pupa wanted these people to learn her language because they had been so nice to her and her son. She had come to have a great affection toward these white people.

Hal worked the garden with Boka, and Hal did the same thing with Boka that Winnie and Sarah were doing with Pupa, and Boka also understood that the white people he was living with, who had rescued him from brutality at his village, were trying to learn his language. Although perhaps eleven years old, Boka knew his language very well and was pleased when Hal would try to pronounce a Tomaka word. Boka no longer laughed when Hal would mispronounce a word; rather he would repeat the word so Hal could pronounce the word correctly.

As time went by, the white people were gaining some knowledge of the Tomaka language. They could even put some short sentences together, which Pupa and Boka would correct if the sentence needed to be corrected. But it would be months and years before these missionaries would be able to share all of God's truth to the Tomaka people. But Pupa and Boka both knew these people had a purpose in mind to learn their language and instinctively felt it to be a good thing.

Eventually these missionaries would learn that *Tomaka* meant "The People." The Fosters no longer used the Morobukuni name for the Tomaka people. As the months went by, the missionaries began to gain more knowledge of the language they were now beginning to learn. Having Sarah, an experienced missionary who had already been working with a tribal language in South America, was helping the Fosters learn the language much quicker than they had been learning earlier, prior to Sarah's coming to be with them.

Pupa and Boka still slept beneath Sarah's room in hammocks, but as time went by, this mother and son had no fear of these people. These people loved them, and Pupa and Boka knew that these white people were safe to be with. But they also realized that these white people had a connection with the spirit world, but not the same spirit world Pupa and Boka had been exposed to with their own people, the Tomaka people. These spirits whom Hal and Winnie and Sarah had contact with were far different from the scary and evil spirits in the Tomaka village. These white people that Pupa and Boka had learned to love had a special relationship with their spirits. The white people's spirits were kind, whereas the Tomaka spirits were scary and evil.

The native mother and son had seen these three missionaries look at these strange leaves, these white leaves with marks on them. They would speak together in the language they spoke, and after some conversation, they would bow their heads and shut their eyes and each in turn would speak in that language that Pupa and Boka had not yet learned. But the mother and son had heard some of those words and knew what some of those words meant. Both the natives and the missionaries were learning a language that was different from their own language.

When Hal and his two fellow missionaries prayed, they also prayed for Pupa and Boka. They prayed that these Tomaka people who lived with them would not be attacked by the evil spirits their tribe had surrendered to. Once Hal prayed (more than once) that if any other of the native people ever came against Pupa and Boka, God would protect Pupa and Boka from those evil spirits.

18
Chapter

Learning God's Way

More and more, Pupa and Boka were drawn into the belief system these white people were honoring. They did not understand the true spirit world, but they knew the spirits that Hal and Winnie and Sarah followed were more loving and caring than their old spirits had been. The spirits of the Tomaka people never helped them. Most of the time, these spirits were evil. They became more and more curious about these spirits their white people were connected to.

They remembered when their own shaman had tried to cast evil spells on Hal and Winnie, that Hal and Winnie were protected by their own spirits against the shaman's evil purpose. They knew that the spirits these white people were following must have more power than the shaman's spirits. Both Pupa and Boka had discussed this before, and both mother and son realized that these spirits they had been bowing down to in the past were evil compared to the spirits Hal and Winnie and Sarah were attached to; the white people's spirits were not evil.

Back at the Tomaka village, the leaders of the village had decided to leave the white people alone, but the shaman of the village wanted to get revenge against the white people who had resisted his spells, which he had tried to put on them. When he failed in casting those spells on them, the shaman, whose name was Morobu, wanted to try again to cast evil spells on those people. During the past year, he had sought power from the demonic forces he used to cast spells on his own people, and Morobu thought he had gained more power that he could use against those white people. But how was he going to cast those spells? He would need to get close to those people to cast his demonic spells.

Morobu came up with a plan. He had strong influence on many of the men in that Tomaka village. He would force some of those men to accompany him to where these white people lived. They would have to take weapons with them, but if his spells worked, they would not be forced to use their weapons. Normally, Tomaka men did not attack other people. They used their weapons for hunting the game they needed to eat. But Morobu also remembered that Pupa and Boka were living with these strange people, and he also wanted to punish Pupa and Boka with his evil spells.

On the next day, Morobu gathered the men he had power over and set out on their way to where Hal and Winnie's home was. It took them several hours to cover the approximately ten miles between the Tomaka village and the Fosters' home.

Morobu planned a time when he and his men would come out of the surrounding jungle to surprise these white people, but he also hoped he could find Pupa and Boka and cast his spells on them so they would get sick and die. He had gained very powerful medicine from the demons who possessed him. Yes, he was a demon-possessed man. That is why he had so much power over those he chose to punish.

When these Tomaka men arrived, Hal and Boka were working out in the garden and the women, Winnie and Sarah, were gleaning more words from Pupa in the shade of the trees near their house. Boka was the first to notice the men from his village, and he also recognized Morobu as the witch doctor who had tried to cast spells on Hal and Winnie.

"Papa Hal!" Look, there are men from our village, and the shaman is with them." Hal heard the "Papa Hal," but he did not understand all that Boka was telling him, but lifting his head, he saw the native men, and he also recognized the witch doctor who had tried to cast spells on him and on Winnie. Hurriedly, Hal and Boka went to the house to protect the women at the house if these men came with an evil purpose. Seeing the shaman, Hal had a foreboding that these men meant harm to them, especially the shaman.

There were seven Tomaka men with the shaman, and they stalked purposely toward the white man's house. They were carrying weapons that Hal could see, and Hal hoped they would not try to annihilate his coworkers and him. When Hal and Boka got near the house, Hal called out to the women so they would know that they were receiving visitors, perhaps visitors with an evil agenda.

When the eight men, which included Morobu, neared the Fosters' house, they stopped just a few yards from Hal, Winnie, Sarah and Pupa and Boka. The first thing the shaman wanted to do was to make examples of Pupa and Boka. He shouted a curse at the mother and son, but nothing happened to them. He tried again, jangling the bones which were strung around his neck, believing that his spirits would attack Pupa and Boka. But again, nothing evil happened to the mother and son who had been banished from their Tomaka village.

Then Morobu turned his attention to Hal and Winnie and a woman he had never seen before, who was just as white as the people he had met about a year ago. Using the evilest incantation against these white people, Morobu shook his fists at these strangers who had made their presence in his land. Still, nothing happened to these white people. It was just like the year past when he had tried to cast spells on Hal and Winnie. Nothing happened.

Then something unusual happened. A bone, which was a talisman for the shaman hung around his neck, suddenly exploded, sending shards of the bone into the skin of Morobu. Then another bone also exploded, sending more splinters from this last bone into Morobu's skin, and one of the splinters pierced into the shaman's stomach.

The men who were with the shaman realized that the spirits of these white people were much more powerful than Morobu's spirits.

They began to retreat and soon broke into a run that would take them away from these strange white people. They knew then that these white-skinned people had greater spirits than the spirits who had always been a problem to the Tomaka people. As they retreated, going back to their own village, they began discussing what had just happened. Who were these spirits the white people had around them? They were definitely more powerful than the shaman's spirits.

Pupa and Boka were also amazed at what had just happened. They had never seen the shaman being defeated except for last year when the shaman had tried to cast spells on Hal and Winnie. And now Hal and Winnie's spirits protected the mother and son from Morobu's evil spirits. Pupa and Boka were amazed. They needed to try to find out who these good spirits were and why they were willing to protect Pupa and Boka.

Hal, Winnie, and Sarah too, were startled at what had just happened. Would the Lord give them an opportunity to reach out to the Tomaka people, since the witch doctor's magic had failed? But the missionaries were also thrilled at what had just happened. Even Sarah was amazed. Nothing like that had ever happened among the people she was reaching out to in the South American rain forest, nothing like the event she had just witnessed. Hal and Winnie were also amazed that the Lord was willing to protect their extended family from the evil the shaman had planned to do to all of them.

Hal called their group to a time of prayer and this time included Pupa and Boka. The Lord had certainly protected that mother and child, and although they could not understand all the words of prayer these missionaries said, they knew they had been protected by more powerful spirits than the shaman relied upon.

Pupa thought, *Who are these spirits? Why are they more powerful than the spirits that bring evil on the Tomaka people?* Pupa now understood that these white people with whom she lived had come for a purpose. She did not realize their entire purpose, but she knew in her heart that what they had she also wanted to have in her own stomach. (We know these Stone Age people are not stupid; they are just illiterate.) Although Pupa could not understand the entirety of the gospel, she was drawn to this spirit of love. She had never been so at peace in all her life. Could these people who had befriended her and her son explain to her this peace she felt? Even Boka felt about the same way his mother was feeling. And Boka had been shocked when those bones on the shaman's chest exploded. These spirits of these white people were very powerful, but they were also benevolent.

After the prayer time was finished, Sarah went to her supplies and brought a comic book style of printing with pictures, that might help Pupa and Boka understand the Lord of life. As she gathered the mother and son together, they were amazed at the pictures they saw on those colored pages. These pictures told a story, and with the limited Tomaka language Sarah had learned during the past months, Sarah began to share the gospel with Pupa and Boka. And now they actually began to understand it. Now they knew in their stomachs why Hal and Winnie, and also Sarah, had come to their land. And they were thrilled; they were thrilled to finally begin to understand the spirits the white people knew, and they were thrilled that these spirits were kind and benevolent rather than being evil and punishing.

During the time Pupa and Boka had been with the Fosters, and then the last few months with Sarah, the mother and son began to understand some of the words these white people used. Both sides began to understand each other more and more. This learning of language was beginning to be a blessing to all of those who lived together as one family.

Little by little, Pupa and Boka began to grasp parts of the gospel the missionaries were sharing with them. Wasn't it thrilling to know that there was one God who had created the jungle, the ground they lived on, and even the stars and the sea? The more the mother and son learned about this Great Spirit, the more they wanted to know this loving and benevolent God.

19
Chapter

A Tomaka Decision

When the natives who had gone with Morobu returned to the Tomaka village, they began sharing the amazing things they had witnessed. The white people were protected by a power that was greater than the spirits of the Tomaka people. As KamApu and the other village elders learned what had happened to their shaman, Morobu, they began to consider another plan. About a year ago, they had decided that they should leave these white people alone, but now what they were hearing about the shaman's bad experience, they had to gather the leading men together and see if it was wise to leave these strangers alone.

KamApu, Badi, and Koopa gathered the other elders together to talk about these men who had accompanied Morobu to the white people, and the fearful thing that had happened to Morobu. Morobu had violated the decision made by the elders and leaders of their village, but the Tomaka people were extremely troubled by what had happened to their shaman. Morobu made the journey back to their village, but he was hurting from the shards of bone that pricked his skin, and especially that shard that had penetrated his stomach. Even the shaman was fearful of the experience he had endured.

Days passed as the Tomaka villagers were trying to make sense of what had happened to Morobu, but of course, it was Morobu's own fault. He had violated the decision reached the year before by the leaders of the village. In his anger toward the white people who had not succumbed to his spells, he had gathered the group of Tomaka men to shock and trouble these strangers. But that was history now. That had not gone as the shaman had planned.

After more than a week of deliberation, the village elders reached a decision. They had determined to learn more about these white strangers who had come into their land, but the only way they could do that was to move some of their Tomaka people closer to these strangers. The decision was made to move one of the family groups that occupied one of their longhouses somewhat close to these white strangers. They would have to select a site that would work for them, to have a garden site and to have water nearby, and then construct a new longhouse that could house these families. This would move forty to fifty people from their current village to the new location.

It would be KamApu who would be the leader of the Tomaka people moving to a new location, but the other leaders, Badi and Koopa, were in the other longhouses where KamApu did not live. When the time came to build their new longhouse near where the white people lived, it seemed reasonable to the elders of the village that it should be KamApu's longhouse people that would move to the new location. KamApu had already met the white people and had been friendly with them, and they also were friendly with KamApu and the younger men with him.

The Fosters and Sarah had no idea of what the Tomaka people were planning, and they were extremely surprised when they noticed some of these people, all of which were men, exploring the valley near the stream that flowed by the Fosters' house. They were not really that near; they were perhaps three quarters of a mile or even an entire mile from the missionaries' location. But the Fosters, Sarah, and Pupa and Boka knew that something unusual was going on. What were these Tomaka people doing?

As a few days went by, the missionaries noticed that the natives were beginning to build some kind of structure, and as more days went by, they could tell that the natives were building a longhouse. What had caused this decision? Were the Tomaka people moving their entire village to this new location? As Hal, Winnie, and Sarah discussed this, they hoped that they would have an opportunity to minister to these natives since they would be nearby.

That is what the Fosters had been hoping for since the very beginning of their time on Morobuku Island. They had discussed moving their location near the Tomaka village, but then the incident with Pupa and Boka had changed their thinking, knowing that they would have to keep Pupa and Boka away from that village for some time. But now it seemed that the Tomaka people were moving close to them. God had been making a plan for these missionaries to be closer to these native people so they would have an opportunity to tell them of God's love for them.

In the meantime, Sarah had enabled Pupa and Boka to begin to understand that God loved them and that Jesus had given His own life to rescue them. It was the pictures in that little book that enabled these natives to understand. These pictures told the story that words could not tell. In those pictures, they could see Jesus and what Jesus endured when He suffered for them. What thrilling news this was to that mother and son, that the Creator of the world could actually love them and give them an opportunity to love Him. They certainly believed in this Great Spirit. They could tell that He was much more powerful than the spirits that they had been afraid of for so long.

In so many of the Stone Age people cultures, women were not allowed to learn anything about the gods these people worshipped. Only the men could know of the gods they served, and the gods they served were in most ways evil. The demons had made themselves the gods of these people, just as Satan had wanted to take the place of the Creator of the universe. These demons wanted these people to fear them, and fear them they did, because these evil spirits had caused so much pain and heartache to these natives.

But now Pupa had learned that God loved women as much as He loved men. Pupa, in her own language, said, "I would give my own life for that One who gave His own life for me. I want to follow Him all of my life." Sarah did not understand every word Pupa had said, but she knew basically what Pupa was saying, and Boka knew exactly what his mother had said because he spoke his mother's language. Boka was extremely excited that his own mother was giving herself to this Great Spirit because Boka wanted to do the same thing his mother was doing. Boka also spoke up: "I want to do the same thing my mother wants to do. I want to follow the Great Spirit with my whole life."

Sarah, Hal, and Winnie had learned enough of the Tomaka words to understand that Pupa and Boka were giving themselves to Jesus. This mother and son would be their first converts led to Christ. Their hearts were given to the Lord. If the Tomaka people would allow Pupa and Boka back into their midst, these new converts could share the gospel of Christ to their own people. If that happened, they could rescue their people from the demonic spirits that troubled them so.

As the missionaries watched the longhouse being built across the valley from their own home, they could tell that through the weeks that it took for the longhouse to be built, the longhouse would soon be ready for occupancy. And then they saw a sight that gave them hope. Here came KamApu walking toward them with the three younger friends who had visited them more than a year before. As KamApu and his friends neared the house, Hal, Winnie, and Sarah went out to meet them. They wanted them to feel that these friends were welcome at their house. The missionaries brought some food for these visitors, and the visitors were glad to see the food as a welcome gift.

When the Tomaka men were seated on a log that had been placed near the firepit Hal had created, the missionaries sat on another log, facing their visitors. As KamApu began making signs with his hands, he also spoke, and now these missionaries could understand most of what KamApu was saying. They had learned so much from Pupa and Boka the words of the Tomaka people.

KamApu spoke about the shaman and the other men that had visited them several weeks earlier. These men came back to the Tomaka village and told what had happened to Morobu when the shaman had tried to cast his evil spells on these white people and had even tried to cast his evil spells on Pupa and Boka. They had told what had happened to the shaman when the bones on his chest exploded, injuring him. As they told these stories to their own villagers, the leaders of their village were shocked and realized that the spirits of the white people were greater than the spirits the Tomaka people had been following for many generations.

KamApu then asked a question: "Would it be permissible for our Tomaka people to live near you so we could learn more about your greater spirits?" KamApu did not realize that most of what he said was understood by these white people. Hal stepped forward to KamApu and extended his hand to this wizened leader of the Tomaka people. He reached forward and grasped the leader's forearm and leaped into the air, just like KamApu had leaped the first time they had met. As Hal leaped, he shouted the phrase he had heard when they first met, "Maba-ha'-hu," and KamApu shouted the same thing, grinning all the time.

Hal spoke with his limited vocabulary of the Tomaka language, "We would like for you to live nearby. We would like to tell you about our Great Spirit. We can be special friends."

KamApu was surprised that Hal could speak in the native tongue. "How did you know our language?" KamApu asked.

Hal replied, "It was because we have had Pupa and Boka with us for these seasons."

"Ah, ah, ah," KamApu spoke, and the three young men with him said the same thing, "Ah, ah, ah." They were all amazed.

"We plan to move one of our longhouse families to the new longhouse we are building near you," KamApu explained. "In a few more suns, we will bring our families to our new home. Some we will have to carry because they cannot make the journey, but we will not leave them behind to live in another longhouse."

"Are they unable to walk because they are weak, or because they are sick?" Hal asked.

"They have been weak and sick for many days," KamApu replied.

Hal said, "I want to tell you that we have Sarah with us now," pointing to Sarah.

"Saura," said KamApu.

"Sarah may be able to help some of your sick people," Hal replied.

"Ah, ah, ah," cried KamApu.

Then Hal said to KamApu, "Will there be angry things said to Pupa and Boka?" And Hal tried to speak in the Tomaka language. He did not get it all correct, but KamApu understood what Hal was trying to say.

KamApu replied, "Boka violated one of our sacred places because he had not yet been taught about the sacred places. He was too young to know, and that is why his father banished him and his mother from our village. But since we learned that your spirits protected them from the shaman's curse, we will be kind to Pupa and Boka. We do not want to anger your more powerful spirits." That was a long phrase for Hal to digest, but Winnie and Sarah also heard, and the three of them could make sense of what KamApu had said. Pupa and Boka knew exactly what KamApu said, and they would tell the missionaries what KamApu said, word by word.

With forearm gripping, and leaping and shouting, laughing all the time, the Tomaka men returned on their way to go to their own village. It had been a good interview with the Tomaka men, and it was also a thrilling interview for the missionaries. Now their God was answering their prayers. They would finally be able to acquaint the Tomaka people with the God who had made the universe, their own land, and who had created them also. This was what the missionaries had come for, to share God's love and His hope to people who had never heard of Him before.

Later, Boka would speak to Hal, his new father figure, about the shaman and what the shaman had done in their village. This time, Boka spoke in the English language. Sometimes children learn a new language quicker than adults can learn a new language. Boka said, in English, "Papa Hal, Morobu did bad our people. He a bad one. He want people fear his power. He make people sick with bad spells. But your spirits made Boka and mother safe."

When Hal heard Boka speak in English, Hal became ecstatic. "Boka, you have learned our language well. You can help us to learn your Tomaka language, and you can speak Jesus's message to your own people, if you are willing to do that."

Boka said, "Will my people listen a boy who not become man?"

Hal replied, "We will let God decide that. He wants your people to learn about Him, and how He loves them. Maybe God will cause them to listen to this boy whom God had protected from the shaman."

When Hal, Winnie, and Sarah were together in the living area of their home, Hal said to the ladies, "Boka speaks English pretty well. He has learned our language much quicker than we have learned his."

Sarah answered, "Yes, we had the same experience with the Tunebo children in South America. They learned our language much quicker than the adults did although we never tried to teach the adults our language. The children would listen when we missionaries spoke together in English and began to understand what we were saying. In fact, sometimes the children were better at teaching us their own language. I believe it was God's foresight that you were to adopt Pupa and Boka into your family."

Now the Fosters and Sarah had great hope that they would be able to share the gospel with the Tomaka people much sooner than they had previously thought. It seemed that the Lord had put His stamp of approval on this ministry.

20
Chapter

The Longhouse

About a week after the Tomaka men had left the missionary compound, Hal and Boka noticed people coming toward the longhouse. It was too far for them to recognize who were first coming, but there seemed to be a number of men, carrying bundles of supplies they would need in their new location. Boka said, "Papa Hal, can I go them, see what they do?"

Hal replied, "No, Boka, we must wait until they come to us, and we believe that soon they will come to us." And with that, Hal and Boka continued gathering the food from their garden.

When Hal and Boka brought their garden produce to the house, Sarah and Winnie were still working with Pupa to make progress on learning the language of the Tomaka people. Hal made the announcement that they had seen more activity at the longhouse. The men seemed to be bringing supplies to their new location, and Hal guessed that it would not be long until the new village would be occupied with all their people. Then Hal suggested that they should have another prayer circle, including Pupa and Boka. Both Pupa and Boka had learned some of the language of the white people they were now living with and could understand some of the words these people used when praying. They knew they were reaching to their Great Spirit.

Hal began their prayer session. "Lord, we believe You are giving us an opportunity to share Your good news to these people to whom You have sent us. It was Your leading that brought us here. May we have the wisdom, Your wisdom, to reach out to these people with Your love. May we help them learn about You, and Your love for them."

Then Winnie continued the prayer. "Father, we know You want the Tomaka people to learn of Your grace and Your forgiveness. Please help us to get better with their language so we can share with them the hope that You have given through Jesus."

Sarah continued in prayer: "Lord, we are Your servants, sent here by You to reach out to these people with that gospel You have made available to all the people of the world. We know that You love all nations, all ethnic groups, and even people who have never heard of You. Help us, Lord, to be Your best servants."

Then, surprisingly, Boka joined in the prayer. He had understood most of what these missionaries were saying. Boka prayed in the language the white people used: "Great Spirit, You greater than evil spirit. Get evil spirit away from Tomaka. You powerful!"

Even Pupa was startled that her son had joined in the prayer. The missionaries were also surprised that Boka had prayed in broken English. As they realized that Boka was learning their own language, it would be a great blessing for the boy to help them translate God's message to his own people.

This thrilled the three missionaries. Young eleven-year-old Boka had learned and understood their language, and he could help them learn the Tomaka language much quicker. Boka's mother was also eager to help these white people learn the Tomaka language, these people who had adopted her and her son into their own family.

It was about a week later that the people at the Fosters' home could tell that the Tomaka people had already occupied their long-house. Should they go to them, or should they wait for the Tomaka people to come to them? It was decided that it might be best to wait for the natives to come to them, rather than push these people with perhaps an unwelcome visit. In the meantime, everyone at Grandview prayed that they could meet these people in God's perfect timing. Even Pupa was beginning to utter short prayers to the Great Spirit who had protected her and her son from the demonic presence of the shaman, and sometimes Pupa tried to use the white people's language, but she was much more fluent in the Tomaka tongue. Could the Great Spirit even understand the Tomaka tongue? She would have to ask Mama Sarah about that.

Another week later, there came a few men from the Tomaka longhouse toward the missionary home. As Hal and the rest of the family saw them coming, they could tell that KamApu was coming toward them, and they were ready to welcome KamApu and his fellow tribesmen when they arrived. Pupa and Boka recognized the other men with KamApu, but they hid themselves in case these men wanted to punish Boka and his mother.

As these men approached, Hal gave the greeting he had learned earlier: "Maba-ha'-hu." These men repeated that same greeting to Hal and the ladies who worked with Hal. As they came near, Hal motioned for them to sit on the log where KamApu had sat on his previous visit, and these native men sat. Then Hal, Winnie, and Sarah sat on the facing log. KamApu then spoke. "Hal, you say your woman Saura can help our sick people. We have brought some sick ones to our new longhouse. Can Saura help?" As KamApu spoke he also used the sign language they had used before. He did not know that these white people could understand most of what he asked.

Hal responded after glancing at Sarah, "Yes, we will come to your longhouse. We want to help your people." And Hal also used the sign language to help communicate his answer. "Is it all right to bring Boka along so he can speak our words to you?"

KamApu replied, again using sign language, "Boka is free to come. He is welcome."

As Hal, Winnie, and Sarah prepared to walk the trail to the Tomaka longhouse, Sarah gathered some of the supplies she thought she might need to help these ailing people. She had asked Harold Gray to bring her some vials of penicillin, and Harold had brought them to her on his last supply trip. This may be what these ailing natives needed, but Sarah was not certain of that. Boka was willing to accompany them to the longhouse, and he had been excited to be able to speak to his own people again. When the missionaries arrived at the new longhouse, KamApu led them to a man who was definitely ill. Through Boka, Hal asked, "Was this man a victim of Morobu?"

KamApu replied, "No, he is just feeling bad."

As the missionaries went near the man lying on a hammock, they could tell that this man was ill. Did he have malaria or some other tropical disease? They asked KamApu if it would be all right to put something into the man's arm. The man was asleep and had been asleep for over two days.

KamApu replied, "Help this man. If you do not help him, he will die." Having given permission KamApu noticed a sharp thorn Sarah was putting into the man's arm. Did it hurt the man? Being asleep, the man, whose name was Poromu, did not feel the sharp thing go into his arm. KamApu thought, *Why did Poromu not wake up when the sharp thing stung him?*

Sarah, knowing a few words of Tomaka language, spoke to KamApu. "We would like to come tomorrow to see if the man is getting better."

KamApu was surprised that Saura could speak some of the Tomaka words. KamApu said, "Yes, yes. Come tomorrow to see if Poromu is better."

The new longhouse did not smell like the older longhouses at the village site because this was newly constructed with new palm thatch on the roof and a bamboo floor that did not yet have filth on it. The Tomaka people did not understand that dirt and filth could cause them to become ill. Some of the time, in the middle of the night, they would come out of their hammocks and relieve themselves on the floor rather than going outside to do their business. So far, this new longhouse did not smell like the old longhouses in their previous village. Sarah and Winnie wondered if they could tell these people that they needed to do their bathroom chores outside of their house. Also, Sarah would like to teach these people to bury their excrement using a digging tool and cover it with dirt. There would be so much to do to keep these people healthier. Sarah and Winnie hoped there would be a way to teach these people to be cleaner.

The Fosters and Sarah and Boka then left the longhouse and returned to their own home, which was about three quarters of a mile away from the longhouse. KamApu was hopeful that what Saura had done to Poromu would help Poromu become well, but KamApu knew nothing of the white man's way of making people better. Hal had told KamApu that Saura might be able to help their sick people, and KamApu hoped that was true. KamApu was beginning to trust these strange people.

On the next day, Hal, Winnie, and Sarah returned to the longhouse to see if Poromu had become better. When they went into the longhouse, Poromu was sitting up in his hammock. He was not completely well yet, but KamApu had told him that the white woman had come and stuck something into his arm. Poromu could feel the little sore spot on his arm, but he was feeling much better.

Then KamApu led the missionaries to another person who was ill, again lying in a hammock, but this woman was awake. When she saw these white people, she was showing fear of them, but KamApu told her that they were there to help her. As Sarah looked at the woman, Sarah could tell that she had something different from what Poromu had been suffering from. This time, Sarah brought some tablets out of her medicine bag and suggested that this woman should try to swallow these things. Again, Sarah used Tomaka words, and the woman was surprised to hear a white woman use her own words even if she did not pronounce all the words correctly. But she did understand what Sarah was saying. She swallowed the pills, and Sarah asked someone to give the woman a drink of water.

Would Sarah's ministry in medicine enable the missionaries to share the good news of the gospel of Christ to these people? Time would tell, but it seemed that these people were accepting the presence of these white people.

21
Chapter

Great Spirit Questions

The Tomaka people had seen that the shaman had not been able to cast his spells on the white people who had come to live near them. Also they had heard that Morobu had been hurt when two bones broke apart into splinters. Morobu was not one in the new longhouse, but he had been a shaman, one who could speak to spirits and could cause Tomaka people to die if Morobu chose to do so. Morobu many times was an angry man and could punish people he did not like. But after the bones had splintered into Morobu's skin, the shaman had done no harm to any people in any of the three longhouses. Did the shaman have no power, or was it his decision to not harm people anymore? Most of the Tomaka people were wondering about the shaman they had feared so much.

When the Tomaka people in KamApu's longhouse moved to the new longhouse near the white people, these people were glad that Morobu did not come with them. He did live in one of the other longhouses, but Morobu had always done what Morobu wanted to do. What a relief most of KamApu's people felt when the shaman did not come to live in their new longhouse.

The Tomaka people were curious about why the shaman's spirits were weaker than the white people's spirits. The shaman's spirits had always been strong enough to cause harm to the Tomaka people. The shaman used his spirits many times against the people who did not do what Morobu had wanted them to do. Morobu was a man to be feared, but since the time the shaman's spirits failed him, Morobu had been seen less and less around the Tomaka people. Should the Tomaka people ask about the spirits who seemed to protect the white people who had come to live near them?

The missionaries had seen what had happened to the shaman when Morobu tried to bring his wrath upon them. They had seen how troubled Morobu was when the bone talismans he had around his neck exploded and caused the shaman harm. They had also seen all the men who had accompanied the shaman run away when the men witnessed what had happened to the shaman. Would this give the missionaries an opportunity to share the truth with the Tomaka people about the Creator of the universe, and their island home, and had even created the Tomaka people? They hoped they would be able to share that good news to these natives as soon as possible.

After Sarah had helped the two people in the new longhouse to get better, Pupa and Boka decided it was time for them to make that journey to the longhouse that had been built near them. They had heard what KamApu had said, that they would not be harmed if they came to the longhouse. Pupa was eager to visit with the women of the new longhouse, her old friends. She had been away from her friends for more than a year, and she wanted to be with these friends again. She and her son had not lived in KamApu's longhouse in the old village, but she knew all of these women. She wanted to visit with them. She wanted to hear the gossip these women could share with her, so she and Boka went down the new beaten path to their neighboring longhouse.

When Pupa and Boka arrived at the longhouse, many people who had not seen them during the past year were actually pleased to see them. KamApu had explained to the men of the village that Boka should be treated well by everyone, both the men and the women. And of course, the children who had played with Boka were excited to finally see Boka come to them.

Pupa had a joyous time getting to spend time with her old friends. These women were so excited to be able to see Pupa, and they chattered so much that the men of the longhouse decided to go outside to get some relief from that chattering. And the children gathered around Boka to find out what he had been doing during the time he had been away from them.

It was Boka that began to tell the other children about the God he had been hearing about from the white people who had taken him and his mother into their home. The children were flabbergasted by what Boka was telling them: There is a God who designed and created the world; the same God created the land they lived in; the same God created all the creatures, the birds, and animals they knew; and the same God created the Tomaka people.

When Boka was telling the other children about the God of the universe, there were other boys listening who had already been initiated into the man's world, the world where older boys were taught about the sacred places and about the spirits that lived in those sacred places. The older boys knew that Boka had violated one of those sacred places, and that was why Boka's father had banished him from the village. But these older boys also had heard how the white people's spirits had protected Pupa and Boka and also the white people from the shaman Morobu. This God Boka was speaking about had more power than the spirits of their sacred places and the spirits Morobu used against the people the shaman was persecuting. These older boys were troubled by what they had heard from Boka. Is there really a spirit that powerful?

When the men escaped the chatter of the women, Pupa began telling the other women about the Great Spirit she had learned about from the white people she had been living with. Pupa had learned enough of the white people's words to be able to know what they were talking about. Boka had learned quicker than Pupa had, but both Pupa and Boka had come to believe in the Great Spirit who protected these white people. The Great Spirit had also protected Pupa and Boka when the shaman, Morobu, had tried to cast evil spells on them.

The Tomaka women were shocked that Pupa was telling them of spirits. In the Tomaka world, women were not supposed to know about spirits nor about the sacred places where these spirits dwelt. This was only for the Tomaka men. Should these women even be listening to Pupa as Pupa was telling them about the Great Spirit whom the white women referred to as Father?

And then, Pupa spoke of the Great Spirit's Son who came to earth to live as a human. This Son of the Great Spirit came to the other humans and loved them, and then He gave His own life. He was tortured to death, but then He rose from the dead to go to His Father's place. As Pupa told this story to the women, these women were extremely troubled with what Pupa was telling them. Should they put their fingers in their ears so they could not hear what Pupa was saying? No, they wanted to hear everything Pupa was telling them.

Later in the longhouse, when the children went to their hammocks, the adult men and women heard the children talking about the Great Spirit Boka had been telling them about. These people already knew there was something special about the white people who had come to live near them, and they already knew how the white people's spirits had protected them from the shaman's evil magic. What were they to think about this? Many of the adult men who heard the children talking about what Boka had told them gained very little sleep that night. They were wondering, *Who is this Great Spirit? How much power does this Great Spirit have? Is he really much more powerful than all the Tomaka sacred places where dwelt the Tomaka spirits?* Of course, the men did not know that Pupa had already shared similar information to the women that Boka had told their children. The men thought it would be bad to give this information to their women.

The next day, the men of the longhouse met with KamApu. KamApu had also heard what the children were saying, the things that Boka had told them. These men were troubled. They wanted to talk to KamApu about this situation. What should they do? Should they do nothing, or should they go to the white stranger to find more about this Great Spirit? The men spent all the hours of the morning discussing their situation. Finally, a decision was made. They should send KamApu and their wisest men to talk to the white man that very day.

KamApu chose four men to go with him to talk to Hal. They were not aware that the white women who were with Hal also knew so many things about the Great Spirit. Things of the spirit were forbidden to the Tomaka women, and these men thought that was a universal principle, even in the white man's world.

As the five men approached Hal's house, they called for Hal to come and meet with them. As Hal came to meet with these men he asked, "May I bring Boka with me also? He can make sense of what you say and what I say." Grudgingly, the men agreed that Boka could accompany Hal to their meeting because they knew that Boka had learned the white man's language. The troubling thought to them was that Boka had never been taught about the spirits of the Tomaka people. He had not yet reached the age when the men taught their sons about the spirit world, and that is why when Boka had violated a sacred place, that the boy's father had banished Boka and Pupa from their village.

As the five men met with Hal and Boka, they had a question to ask Hal. Why was Hal's spirit stronger than the Tomaka spirits? Hal had already prayed about how to answer such a question. He was hoping these Tomaka men would ask such a question. Using young Boka as his interpreter, Hal told of the Great Spirit who created the land and the seas and even created the stars, the moon, and the sun. This Great Spirit, referred to by Hal as God, had also created the animals and even man, *The People*.

KamApu had already heard what the children were saying about what Boka had said to them, and they wondered if this was just a child thing Boka was making up, but when Hal was saying the same thing that Boka had shared with their children, these men were surprised and troubled. Why had they never known that there was a Great Spirit who had created everything, and even *The People*.

Hal then, through Boka's translation, shared about the God who had created the stars, the sun and moon, and had also created the earth and its people. Hal tried to keep his explanation as simple as possible so these men could understand about God. "In the very beginning, when God created the first man and woman, there was another spirit that God had also created. But this spirit turned against the God who had made him. He wanted to replace God with himself. Then evil came to the man and woman God had created." Boka did a very good job of translating Hal's words into Tomaka words.

Hal continued: "Through many families, even down to today, the evil spirit hurt these people with his hate. But God never ignored His people. Many, many families ago, God sent His own Son to earth to become a human, just like we are. This Son of God taught the people God's ways, and then this Son of God was put to death by men who did not believe Him. But three days later, God's Son, Jesus, rose from the dead and became alive again. Jesus forgave those who had put Him to death, and Jesus wants to forgive every person, man, woman, and child who will believe in Him and follow His ways."

Boka did a good job of translating Hal's words into the Tomaka words. These men understood what Hal had said through Boka's translation, but Boka could not say "Jesus" the way Hal said it. The Tomaka people had different syllables than the American white people used. Boka said "Heesus" to say the Savior's name, and Hal heard that and made a mental note of how to speak the name of Jesus in the Tomaka tongue.

KamApu said, "Why Heesus die like that? He God's Son. He had power. Why He die?"

Hal replied, and Boka translated: "God loves His people. Heesus loves His people. The only way God can forgive is if someone dies for the evil people do to each other. And Heesus died for us so we can be forgiven. Heesus loves you and your people. Heesus died for you. But he now is with His papa God. He is alive."

KamApu exclaimed, "Ah, ah, ah," and the men with him said the same thing. They had heard and understood what Hal had been saying to them through the boy, Boka. They would have to think about the things Hal had told them. And think about it they did, and they talked together during their walk to their longhouse village. One of the older wise man said, "We have never heard anything like this before." And the other men agreed with him. They had to process this in their minds. Should they immediately share this new idea with the other men in their village? Maybe they should

115

go off together to discuss this among themselves. That is what they decided to do. They made a camp in the middle of the jungle, and far enough, away from their new village so that the other men would not spy on them and hear what they were discussing together. These men had a lot to think about. They would have to decide what to do with this new information.

22
Chapter

Prayer Time

After the Tomaka men left, Hal went to Winnie, Sarah, and Pupa to tell them that they all need to pray for the Lord's guidance on how to share God's truth to these Tomaka people. Pupa and Boka were already believers in Heesus. Pupa had already told Winnie and Sarah about her long visit with the women in the longhouse, that she had told them about Heesus, and His Father. She had told these women, who had never been told by the men of their village about anything having to do with the spirit world. These women knew they were not supposed to know anything about the spirit world. They had no privilege to that knowledge; only the men had that privilege.

The women of the longhouse were completely dumbfounded by the stories Pupa was telling them about a Creator God and about His Son the Father had sent to be a human. They were shocked when Pupa told them that the Great Spirit's Son gave His own life to be a blood sacrifice, to forgive humans of their own rebellion against the Great Spirit. They were also thrilled and shocked that Pupa told them that the Great Spirit's Son rose from the dead and rejoined His Father in the spirit world. Pupa was telling these women about God's love for them. Would they believe her? At least some of them did.

Boka also told that he had shared the same stories with the children, and the children were excited to hear these stories. Were these stories fables, or were they the truth? The older boys who were hearing what Boka was telling, these older boys who had already been told by their fathers and the older men in their village about the spirits in the sacred places, wondered about Boka's stories about the Great Spirit and His Son. But the seed had been planted, and in some of those hearts, the seed began to grow.

Hal and the rest of their group gathered together to discuss and pray about the gospel Hal, Pupa, and Boka had shared with these primitive people. They knew that this new gospel, which these Stone Age people were hearing, had to be troubling to these people. They had never heard anything like this before. Will they accept this gospel, or will they reject it? If they reject this gospel then Hal, Winnie, and Sarah might be in for some persecution, and even death, although from the information they had gathered about the Tomaka people, no outsiders had ever been put to death by these Stone Age people. They might just move back to their old village and ignore the white people who had come to their land.

All these missionaries prayed together for the Lord's best wisdom. How were they going to respond to these people if they accepted the good news of the Lord's gospel? How were they going to reach out to these people if they decided to reject the message that Hal, Pupa, and Boka had shared with them? There were tears falling as these fervent prayers were being lifted up to heaven. Pupa and Boka had been in some of these prayer sessions before, but this time, they could tell that this was an extremely serious prayer time. Pupa and Boka were hoping with all their hearts that their own Tomaka people would believe and respond to the message these white people had come to bring to them. Pupa and Boka knew that the reason these people had come to their land was to bring hope and joy to the Tomaka people; Pupa and Boka already had that hope and joy in their own hearts. They had become followers of Heesus.

A day and a night passed after that special prayer session. Then another day and a night passed before the missionaries heard from any people from the longhouse. It was a difficult waiting period for the missionaries and the two Tomaka people who were living with them.

At the longhouse, some of the women began leaking the information that Pupa had been telling them about the Great Spirit. The men began to realize that these women, who according to the Tomaka custom were not supposed to have any knowledge of the spirit world, had already been told about the spirit world. After KamApu and the other four men who had spent a night in the jungle, discussing what they should do with this new information, a few of the men of the longhouse came to them when they came back and told them that Pupa and been telling the women about the spirit world, especially about the Great Spirit. KamApu and the elders he had with him were surprised, but not too surprised, for they had seen that Pupa and Boka had lived with the white people for more than a year. Boka had also seemed to believe what Hal was saying to KamApu and the elders who had gone to speak with Hal.

The elders of the village realized that they needed to gather all the men together for a large meeting to discuss what they should do with this new information. Even the women had heard about the Great Spirit. Everyone had heard about Morobu, the shaman, having no power over the white people, and he also had no power over Pupa and Boka. And the unbelievable thing happened to Morobu. His own talismans had exploded and sent shards of the bones into Morobu's skin and into his stomach. This Great Spirit the white people knew was much more powerful than the spirits the Tomaka people had served and bowed down to for all the generations they could remember.

As all the men gathered, it was KamApu's turn to speak. He was the most respected leader of the Tomaka people in their new longhouse. When KamApu stood, there was silence in the entire group of men. They were curious about what KamApu would say to them. Did the other elders who had accompanied KamApu to the white people's house agree with KamApu?

When KamApu spoke, every man listened. They needed to know what the elders had decided when they had gone into the jungle to be alone, to discuss the situation they now had before them. Then KamApu spoke:

"We, the elders, have been discussing what we need to do with this new information we have been hearing about the spirit world. It seems that the spirits we have been fearing are not as powerful as the new Great Spirit we are now hearing about. We have talked through the day and night about how to respond to this new information. Morobu had no power over the spirits of the white people. He had no power over Pupa and Boka. That has never before happened. Our shamans have always been able to use the spirits to punish the people they wanted to punish. Some of those people died from the spells the shamans used against them. These spirits had power, but now it seems that they have no power over the spirits of the white people.

"We the elders have made a decision. We must allow the white people to come and tell us about the Great Spirit. Hal, the white man, told us that the Great Spirit made everything we now see. He made the sun, the moon, and the stars. He even made the first man and the first woman. But the evil spirit told them lies, and they began to die because of the evil spirit. Our spirits, which we have obeyed, have not been kind to us. They have punished us. They have made some of our people die. When Saura came and pierced Poromu's arm, on the next day, Poromu was much better. Poromu is here now in our group of men. Poromu is well again. Again, Saura gave one of our women who was ailing something to swallow. The woman swallowed the things Saura gave her, and in two days, she was much better.

"These white people want to tell us about the Great Spirit and His Son, Heesus. These appear to be good spirits, not bad spirits. But the white people also want to tell our women and children about the Great Spirit. The elders of our village have made a decision. Even the women and the children shall hear the white people's stories. This has never been done before among the Tomaka people, but we think everyone should hear about the Great Spirit. We will choose a day and gather every Tomaka person to hear the white people tell us about the Great Spirit… That is all we have to say to you."

23

Chapter

The Gathering

The elders sent a messenger to the Fosters' house to tell them that they are allowed to come to the village and tell them about the Great Spirit, not just the men but all the people of the village, women and children included. It would be two days from this day. That day would be Sunday, the Lord's Day.

How excited the Fosters and Sarah were that they were going to be able to tell the Tomaka people about God's love for them and God's willingness to cleanse them from all the bad things they had ever done. They could have eternal life in a heaven they had never even imagined if they believed God's truth and if they follow His way and His morals. What an opportunity the Lord had given them.

Sarah was so excited. It had taken a few years for the missionaries in South America, working with a new tribe, to be able to share the gospel with a large group of people. The Fosters had been on the Morobuku Island for only a year and a half, and Sarah had been there for only six months. Again, what an opportunity the Lord had given them, to share hope and gladness and salvation to these Tomaka people. The Lord had convinced Hal and Winnie to become missionaries to Papua New Guinea, and the Lord had sent them to a people who had never heard about God, but not in Papua New Guinea. He had sent them to an island that most of the world knew nothing of. He had sent them to share God's good news to these Tomaka people. And Pupa and Boka were also excited. They had come to believe the gospel of the Lord Jesus Christ. They had become so happy to hear about Heesus who had given His own life in order to rescue them for eternity. And now they were going to be able to share that good news with their own people.

When the day arrived for the missionaries and Pupa and Boka to go to the village, they were surprised that there were more people there than the longhouse could hold. Word had been sent to the old village, and many of those people wanted to hear what the white people had to say to them. The old village people had already seen how their spirit had protected them from the shaman's curse, and even Pupa and Boka were protected by the white people's spirit. They had heard about that. They had heard that Morobu had threatened Pupa and Boka, but his curse did not harm them at all. These people from the old village wanted to hear what these people had to say. Many of them came to hear these words.

When Hal, Winnie, and Sarah came to the area of the longhouse, they were shocked that there were over a hundred people there. The capacity of the new longhouse could only hold about fifty people, but apparently, word had traveled to the old village, and most of the people from the old village wanted to hear what these white people would say. Then Hal noticed that Morobu, the shaman, was also there, but he had no talismans hanging around his neck. He seemed different from the last time Hal and Winnie and Sarah had last seen him.

As the group saw the missionaries coming to them, they shouted, "Maba-ha'-hu," that universal greeting word, but when everyone shouted that phrase, it seemed like the missionaries were in a stadium filled with people at a football game in the United States. Hal then leaped in the air and shouted back to the crowd, "Maba-ha'-hu!" And the crowd roared its approval. The crowd was ready to hear what the missionaries had to say.

Then KamApu and the elders of his own longhouse stood before the crowd gathered there, the crowd having formed a large semicircle and seating themselves on the ground. KamApu spoke to the crowd. "We have heard of a Great Spirit who has protected and helped these white people. We want Hal to tell us about this Great Spirit. But also, I need to tell you that Saura was able to heal two of our sick people in our new longhouse. We, elders, believe these white people are good people. Listen carefully to what they say to you today."

When the elders went to sit on the ground with the crowd, Hal then moved to a central location. He wanted everyone to hear what he had to say, and he also motioned for the boy, Boka, to come to his side. He knew Boka could speak the Tomaka language better than Hal could, and Hal wanted everyone to understand what he was telling them.

Again, using young Boka as his interpreter, Hal told of the Great Spirit who created the land and the seas, and even created the stars, the moon, and the sun. This Great Spirit, referred to by Hal as God, had also created the animals and even man…and *The People*. Again, as he had told the five men who had come to learn about the Great Spirit, Hal told how the evil spirit, whom God had created before He created the man and woman, then lied to the man and woman so that they would turn away from God. But Hal made certain that God did not create an evil spirit. The spirit whom God had created decided to turn away from God and began to do evil things.

Then Hal told the crowd of listeners how so many people, down through many generations, had not listened to God when God had sent messengers to them to tell them not to be evil. But the people turned away from God. That is why God decided to send His own Son to rescue the people from their wickedness. The Son of God did many healings so that people would realize that God loved the people, and some of the people believed what the Son of God, Heesus, said to them and began to follow Heesus.

But many did not want to follow Heesus. They wanted to do evil like they had done before God sent His own Son to become a human. And finally, Heesus was killed by the evil people, but the reason Heesus allowed them to kill Him was because there had to be a blood sacrifice to forgive these people of their evil ways. Heesus had the power of God with Him. He could have decided not to rescue these people, but He loved these people and was willing to forgive them. He allowed them to kill Him. But then three days later, Heesus came alive again. Many days after that, after He had taught those who followed Him to share His forgiveness to those who would accept His way, He went up into the sky to live with His Father, the Great Spirit.

Hal then told the crowd that if they believed this story they had just heard, when they died here on their land, if they followed the ways of Heesus, they would live again. They would not live in this world in these bodies but would go just like Heesus had gone to be with the Great Spirit. They would never die again. They would live forever and ever.

And Hal also told the crowd that Heesus had sent him and his wife, Winnie, and had also sent Sarah to tell them this story of God's forgiveness. God loves *The People*. God wants *The People* to love Him also.

After Hal had shared his message through Boka, the crowd was stunned. A few had heard part of this story before, but most of them had never heard anything like this. The crowd was silent for many minutes. They had to process this story Hal had told them in their own minds and in their stomachs. Boka had told them in their own words how God loved them and how He had sent His own Son to rescue them from bad things and to give them eternal life so that after they died their normal death, like they had seen so many of their own people die, they could go to live with the Great Spirit forever and ever, and they would be happy.

One person stood and did not know what to do. It was KamApu. Hal called out to him: "Did you hear the story with your own ears?" And Hal spoke in the Tomaka words.

"Yes! Yes! I heard your words, and I believe your words. I am happy to hear your words. I know your Great Spirit sent you to give us this story. How can I become a follower of Heesus?"

Hal responded, "If you believe in your mind and in your stomach that Heesus is the Son of the Great Spirit and you want to follow Heesus and His ways, you can now become the first follower of your Tomaka people." KamApu strode to Hal and wrapped his arms around Hal, then he picked up Boka and held him at arm's length over his head and shouted, "This child has given us joy today!"

Then others came to Hal and bowed down to him, but Hal raised them to their feet and said, "I am not Heesus! I am just a follower of Heesus. I am not a shaman. I am just a man, like all of your own men. I am just a follower of Heesus!" Then Hal spoke to the people who came to him and said, "There is one more thing to do today. We have a small river nearby (and Boka was translating what Hal said). It is like you will die to your old self, and you will be buried in water like a grave. When you come out of the water, you will be a new person, forgiven by Heesus!"

More than fifty people came to that water that day and accepted Heesus as their Great Spirit. As the days went by more and more people came to be baptized into Heesus, to receive His forgiveness.

There were daily lessons given through Hal, Winnie, and Sarah, using Pupa and Boka as their interpreters. More people began to learn more about the Great Spirit, and less people believed in the old evil spirits anymore. Even Morobu began to come to the daily lessons and finally became a follower of Heesus. The evil spirits were no longer in Morobu.

The months went by and more of the Tomaka people came to believe in Heesus until most of the people in the old village and in the new village had already begun to follow Heesus.

It would take a few years for the missionaries to translate the Tomaka language to be able to give them God's Word in written form. They had begun already to teach these people how to read their own words, and it would take more time to translate the books of the New Testament into the Tomaka language. These missionaries were here for the long haul. They would stay until their work was done.

Then one day, one of the men came to Hal and spoke to him (by this time Hal had become somewhat fluent in the Tomaka language), "Papa Hal, did you know that there are two other villages of Tomaka people in this land?"

Hal was flabbergasted. *We still have a lot of work to do on Morobuku Island*, Hal thought to himself.

About the Author

Daniel was raised on a farm/ranch in Nebraska. He worked with cattle and had broken a few horses at a young age. Both of his brothers went into the military, but Daniel wanted to serve the Lord in a special way. He had earned more than one scholarship to various colleges but chose a Bible College in Scottsbluff, Nebraska. That is where Daniel met his soon-to-be-wife.

Daniel has been in the preaching ministry for fifty-seven years, and since 1992, Daniel has been a director of The Waray-Waray Project in the Philippines, a ministry to a least-reached people group. He has always loved mission work. In 1974 he and his wife were recruited to be missionaries in Brazil, South America, but that was not God's plan for them. Daniel has been preaching minister in six states of the US: Wyoming, South Dakota, Nebraska, Kansas, Texas, and Oklahoma. Over the last forty years, he has served churches in Oklahoma. He has taken five mission trips to Mexico and the Philippines. He and his wife have done their best to serve the Lord in the best possible way.

Daniel has always been mission-minded, and that is what this work of fiction is about, a young couple who have been mission-minded. This book is a work of fiction but speaks to the heart of a mission-minded people.

CPSIA information can be obtained
at www.ICGtesting.com
Printed in the USA
JSHW050501150222
22908JS00001B/72